PAINTING WITH WORDS

BY
FREEZY THE BARBER

WASHINGTON AVENUE PRESS

ISBN: 979-8-9996644-0-2
First Edition
Cover & Interior Design: James A. Freeman
Published by: Washington Avenue Press
Printed in the United States of America

This is a work of poetry. Names, characters, places, and events may be the product of the author's imagination or used in a literary context. Any resemblance to actual persons, living or dead, is purely coincidental.

Dedication

For my late mother, Alma Mae Mack —
You didn't just give me life. You gave me rhythm, voice, and vision. You passed down a gift you didn't even realize you had — the way with words, the poetry in presence, the song in struggle, the art in everyday love. You shaped me into the man, the father, the artist I am. This book is yours as much as mine.

For my late sister Robin "Oowey" McBride — I miss you dearly but I know you're up there bragging about your "little big brother" just like you always did.

For my daughters —
Thank you for reminding me what light looks like. You are the reason I believe in tomorrow.

For my wife —
Thank you for not just supporting me, but actually believing in me. That goes farther than any cheer from the sidelines — that belief moves mountains.

And for every soul who sees themselves somewhere in these pages — this book is for you too.

— Freezy

Table of Contents

The First Layer of Color

Legacy, family, and the quiet power of beginnings

Beneath Her Skin: Storms, Suns & Sacred Roots

Black womanhood in all its pain, glory, and grace

The Chemistry of Us

Where sensuality, intimacy, and soul collide

What We Become

Fatherhood, growth, and the echoes of manhood

Laugh Lines & Sharp Edges

Truth wrapped in comedy, culture, and satire

Intermissions of Thought

Short sparks. Still moments. Tiny revelations.

Final Brushstrokes

Tributes, truths, and the closing statement

Author's Note

This book is more than a collection of poems — it's a living archive of my growth, my memories, my struggles, and my spirit.

Many of these pieces were written over the course of years, in different chapters of my life. Some started as song lyrics. Some lived in the margins of notebooks. Some were stored in my phone, my head, or scribbled on scraps of paper long before they ever had a title. A few were born from pain. Others from joy. All of them, though—**real.**

What you're holding is not the voice of one moment, but the echo of many versions of me. Young me. Searching me. Healing me. Evolving me. These poems are drawn from different seasons, stitched together by truth and time.

This is not just my story. It's a reflection of our stories — of legacy, of love, of laughter, of loss, and of the resilience that carries us forward. I didn't write these to be perfect. I wrote them to be honest.

So dip the brush into your memories—some of this might look familiar. Whether you're here to heal, laugh, cry, or catch a vision—this is *Painting with Words.*
Let's create something beautiful together.

The World to Ourselves

For Alma Mae Mack

It was never just us—
not in that house,
not with twelve kids,
plus bonus cousins, grands, and folks
who needed somewhere to land.

My mother's house was a lighthouse,
always on,
always open.
Her love never turned anyone away.

But I remember the moments
when it felt like it was just us—
like the world shrunk down
to a hotel room in Rhode Island,
Lobster Fest, plates stacked high,
and me, the oldest boy,
brought along not by accident,
but by choice.

We shared the room,
shared the weekend,
shared the silence
that only exists
between two people
who truly see each other.

And before that—
when I was little—
I sat on her bed,
learning to play *I Declare War*
with my small hands,

holding big cards.
She laughed every time I slapped one down like my father.
We had no chips,
but it felt like Vegas and we were bettin' everything.
We giggled with joy that shook the room.
And I can still feel it.

Maybe it was around then—
when I was still light enough
to float in my dreams—
that we danced with glowing reindeer.
Little sparkly things
that lit up the room like fireflies.
She laughed then too.
Maybe it was real.
Maybe it wasn't.
But I've never let go of it.
Some memories are so magical,
they don't care if they happened.

And one night when I was seven I got to stay up late—
school night or not.
All the other kids were in bed,
but Ma let me stay up and draw.
It was for my first poem,
"Ten Cars Parked in the Parking Lot,"
published in a calendar in eighty-nine.
She gave me the good markers.
Not crayons—real magic markers.
We drew busted fenders
and headlights like eyes.

And the whole time, it felt like the world was quiet,
and ours.

She walked the pavement when she had to,
but somehow still held the house down
without ever leaving it.
We never missed school.
We never went looking like we missed love.
She was proud of me—
not just for poems and grades—
but for how I carried myself.
For the man I chose to be.
A family man.
A steady man.
A simple man.

But she was there long before I had words for any of that.
She was there after surgeries when my knee was split open,
torn patella and all— six days in the hospital
when most folks go home the same day now.
She was there with snacks,
with prayers,
with strength
stronger than any medicine.

She was there in the bleachers too—
coaching baseball teams
in full uniform,
cane in hand,
legs aching from the fight rheumatoid arthritis brought upon her
body. But she still showed up
like a general.

Got all us boys on the field
even when the uniforms weren't free,
and the money wasn't there.
She found it.
She made it.
We didn't even get to keep the jerseys,
but we kept the love—for the game, and for our mother.

She raised all those girls—
but my mother was a boy mom
through and through.
Baseball, surgeries, graduations,
barbershop talks,
early-morning doctor's appointments.
She didn't just raise sons—
she stood up for us.
Even from a wheelchair.

And when I sang in the church choir in Harlem,
I caught her eye glisten.
She loved that.

She was a singer herself—
a soloist on the Baptist scene.
Poet, too.
That's where I got it from.
Every word I've ever loved
feels like it first passed through her.
And then came Journey Jane.
Even though they only met in person a few times, they had a bond you
can't count in visits.
My mother used to watch her through video chats for hours,
while I'd run around prepping bottles
or grabbing her food.

They'd sing.
They'd talk.
She'd babysit through a screen,
but the love was in full presence.

She used to sing to her—
"Let Me Call You Sweetheart"—
but made it her own:
"Baby Journey, I'm in love…"
And Journey lit up like she knew
she was hearing royalty.

She still does things that remind me of Ma.
That calm expression.
That soft lean-back while watching TV,
bottom lip tucked in when she's
concentrating. Sometimes I look over
and see my mother sitting in my daughter.
That fat grandma smile,
That's what she called her.
The peace in her face.
It's all there.

But it didn't start with Journey.
Dominae was the first.
Raised right alongside me,
and even when I wasn't there,
she was with my mother—
not waiting on me to come back,
but posted up with her grandma
like it was home base.
Coffee and butter rolls,
their sacred routine.
    hile I went to work.

She told me just the other day as I teased her about the way she
eats, "I'm an Alma Mack baby."
Said it with her whole chest.
And I laughed—
because she is.
She holds her food just like my mother did,
dainty little fingers,
skinny pinky lifted
like royalty never skipped a generation.

My mother had those long, delicate hands—
rings on her fingers like little crowns.
Slim, elegant, and full of grace.
She was a big woman,
but her hands and her face
belonged to a different scale—
pretty, poised, and unforgettable.

It all lives on.
In the pinky.
In the pride.
In both my daughters—
one by blood,
the other by heart—
who are forever Alma Mack babies.

I was her first son.
Her tenth child.
The new beginning
after nine girls
who softened and sharpened her
for the boy she'd raise
into a man.

A simple man.
A husband.
A father.
A builder of home and heart.
Just like she showed me—
not with speeches,
but with example.
Not with instruction,
but with presence.

And yeah—
I think about that Lynyrd Skynyrd song,
the one that always sounded
more like a conversation with my Mom
than Ronnie Van Zandt himself.
"Come sit beside me, my only son…"
I heard oldest son when I played it back in my
head. Because I was.

The first boy after nine girls.
A different kind of miracle.
She may not have said all the words,
but she gave me the wisdom.
In her silence.
In her hands.
In her steady presence.

She taught me how to love a woman,
how to build a home,
how to find God without a pulpit.
How to be a simple man
in a complicated world.

The last time I saw her
was last Mother's Day.
She kissed me—not fast.
Slow, deliberate.

Not goodbye.
But something deeper.
Something eternal.
I walked away full,
and I carry those kisses
like armor now.

People talk about heaven
like it's far away.
But when she looked at me that day,
when she kissed me slow—
I think I touched it.
Just for a second.

Because I know—
my mother's work didn't stop with
me.

It's stretching forward—
through my hands,
into hers.

That's the legacy.
That's the miracle

From boy to man.
From son to father.

From Alma to Journey.

Even now—
in the noise,
in the quiet,
in the memories and the moments that don't
need to make sense
to still be sacred—
I carry this truth
like a whisper I'll never forget:

That even in a crowded house,
with so many voices,
there were moments
when Ma gave me

the world to ourselves — *by her son*

She began.

Then the world responded in nine voices.

Nine Before Me

Nine before me, paving the way,
Born in a world that took more than it gave.
Through streets of struggle, storms of pain,
Yet love and lessons still remain.

My sisters…

The first one we call Tom, strong and tall,
Not a man, yet taught us all—
How to hoop, how to drive,
How to endure a long battle and survive.

A Camaro packed with kids so tight,
Racing to Boston Road at night.
Stricken by the epidemic
An unfortunate plight,
but you got yourself clean and now you all right

Number Two, our Mama Bear,
Fights her battles, says a prayer.
Her home is spotless, floors that shine,
Yet demons linger in her mind.

Project Return, that was her place,
And I still believe she'll win the race.
No matter how long it takes Mama Bear,
I know you've come this far by faith.

Number Three, Our Mom's own name,
Trials and tears, but wisdom gained.
Taught me loss and how to cope
About STDs and how they're no joke

Birds and bees, since I ain't have a dad—
That important conversation she and I had.
And since she backed out of that one-armed fight,
Imma troll her about it till the end of my life.

Number Four showed us the view,
A world so vast, a dream so true.
Lived like stars beyond the gate,
Taught us to reach, not spectate.

From Motown to the NBA,
Showed us all where there is will, there is way.
Reaching goals with more to come,
Not being defined by where you're from.

Number Five, with faith so whole,
Prays for all and saves lost souls.
A minister's heart, a righteous goal,
Her words still echo, make us whole.

Number Six, Princess Peach,
Sweet as honey, yet storms unleash.
She strays at times but not too far,
Love's embrace is where we are.

Yeah I know life was rough, but you're rougher,
You were never an outcast, big sister.
Just hope you're safe and sound—
So get your mind right and stop playing around.

Number Seven held it down,
Kept us fed when Mom left town.

Tough and bold, she made the rules,
Made sure we ate and went to school.

And when Stella left to get her groove,
Who had our back till Mom made moves…
It was you.

Number Eight, our Pretty Bird,
A fighter fierce, her voice still heard.
Oowey, soaring, strong yet free,
Street fights, then cancer's war—she beat.

She shielded us when we were small,
Then we grew tall and fought for all.
Her voice still lingers, loud and bright,
If I could hear it for one more night.

If only I could watch her win one more fight—
That would do my heart just right.
Better place? They could be right.
But you definitely didn't deserve your plight.

And number nine with nine to show.
A legacy that still will grow.
nine roots on Big Alma's tree.
Nine branches added to the ninety three

Through cracks in life, through nights so long,
They stumbled, fell, but still stayed strong.

They raised us close, they showed us truth,
Their missteps shaped and saved our youth.

Nine before me, hands held tight,
Still within our reach, still in the fight.
And whether they knew it, or even tried,
They built these men who stand with pride.

Simple Flowers

For Journey Jane, on your 7th birthday

You're turning seven on a Saturday,
Just like your daddy—same kind of day.
My seventh was on a Sunday, it felt brand new,
Now I see that magic repeating through you.

Your mom is tall—six feet since she was ten,
And you're rising just like her, again and again.
But it's not your height that makes you grand,
It's the voice, the spark, the heart you command.

Journey Jane, you memorize songs
In Spanish, Swahili—you never get it wrong.
K-pop lyrics without speaking the tongue,
How does all that fit in someone so young?

You call Dolly Parton your fairy book mother,
'Cause she sent you books like no other.
You hear her voice at night so true,
And even thought she was speaking directly to you.

At school, you shine with every chance,
You just aced first grade with perfect attendance!
You get every award—except "most improved,"
Because you've been great since you first made your move.

At school, you're a legend in your own way,
Not just for the grades, but the everyday.
Never late, never absent, no early checkouts—
You show up with pride, with zero doubts.

Perfect attendance, year after year,
It's more than a sticker or a loud cheer.

You've learned what grown folks often forget:
That showing up is the safest bet.

I tell you often, and I'll say it again—
Showing up is 90% of the win.
And you show up with grace, head held high,
While others wonder and ask, "How? Why?"

It's who you are. It's what you do.
And every day, I walk in with you.

Stand by that door, watch the kids roll in,
Fist bumps and "Have a great day!" A whole lotta grins.

Some folks may see just a morning chore,
But to me, it's protection—and so much more.
Your presence is purpose. Your light is loud.
And Grandma sees it too—from above the clouds.

She left this earth two days after you turned six,
But not before she saw your birthday mix.
It's like she waited, held off the pain,
So you could keep your joy without the rain.

And when I look at you—I swear it's true—
Sometimes I see her shining through.

Her thoughtfulness, her quiet grace,
That knowing smile upon your face.

This week, I rushed to your school awards, half-aware,
Grabbed some cheap flowers from Food Lion on the way there.

Thought nothing of it—just something to do,
But Journey Jane, then I looked at you…

Your jaw dropped open, your eyes went wide,
You held those flowers like a glowing bride.
You covered your mouth, as your cheeks turned red,
That's when I saw a moment I'll never forget.

It struck me deep—that sacred glow—
A little rite you didn't know.
Your first bouquet from the man you adore,
And I hope it's the first of so many more.

You once said you'd marry me someday,
When you were four and wanted your way.
"But why can't I, if I love you most?"
I held back tears, swallowed the ghost.

I said, "One day, love will come your way,
From someone who chooses you every day."
You frowned and said, "But I choose you,"
And I didn't know what else to do.

I'm glad that phase has come and gone,
But I miss it too—'cause it defined our bond.
You didn't love me 'cause I'm the best,
You loved me because I never left.

Ya see attendance ain't just a schoolhouse goal—
It's showing up, heart, mind, and soul.

And honey, I've tried to never be late
For any moment that helps you feel safe.

Frenchie from *Grease* once said it plain,
"The only man a girl can truly depend on is her daddy," and again,
It ain't always true—but for you, it will be—
Because I'm here for you, eternally.

So blow out your candles, sweet Journey Jane,
You sing like sunshine, you dance through rain.
And just know—through all life's hours—
I saw forever in your simple flowers.

"Candy Sweets"

In the warmth of our kitchen, where love found its seat,
Alma stirred up magic in her candy sweets.
With hands that knew struggle and a heart full of gold,
She turned simple yams into stories untold.

Her candy sweets traveled from our home to the street,
Into local soul food spots, a neighborhood treat.
She made a way out of nothing, a nourishing queen,
Her legacy blossomed from seeds unforeseen.

A nourishing soul, that's what her name meant,
Alma lived it fully, never knowing its intent.
She raised generations, her impact so vast,
From twelve of her own to descendants unsurpassed.

She cared for the children of mothers in need,
Offered them refuge and a place to be freed.
In Apartment 8F, Big Alma reigned,
With candy sweets and love unchained.

Local spots sought her signature dish,
Her candy sweets a community wish.
From our humble home to the city's embrace,
She spread her love, leaving a sweet trace.

She never knew kin but the family she grew,
A legacy built from the love that she knew.
Her candy sweets weren't just a dish on a plate,
They were poems of resilience, a testament to fate.

I try to recreate that taste, that embrace,
But it's her soul in the sweetness that can never be replaced.
Now my own candy sweets carry her flame,
A legacy of love that will always remain.

Now That You're Both There

I bear your first name, Dad, but not your line—
Freeman I am, and I wear it just fine.
Still, I wonder, when I sign my name,
Am I half a legacy, or part of your shame?

Was it pride? Was it doubt? Was it fear in your head
That made you deny your own son, instead?
Mom said you swore we weren't your three boys,
Like she'd been flirting with every man who made a noise—

The mailman, the housing man, and anyone near.
Your age made you bitter, your heart full of fear.
She was young, beautiful, with fire in her step,
And you let suspicion destroy what was left

Ma, you stayed long, fought through every storm,
Raised twelve kids and some of their kids on scraps, but kept us fed and warm.
The girls recall they knew cold—no lights, no heat,
On Bryant Ave., surviving with times bare minimum to eat.

But by the time us boys came through,
The projects came with a different view.
Utilities included, that was the grace,
A little more light but in a much darker place.

We didn't freeze or sit in the dark,
But still bore struggle, still bore the mark.
We came upstairs when the streetlights came on,
Just to be safe before the dark went long.

Dad, I don't recall a particular day you walked away,
No slamming door that marked your stay.
You just weren't really "there," not by choice or plan,
But I just don't remember you being that man.

You left this earth when I was just a boy,
One month from twelve, and it stole my joy.
Jose Canseco had a fly ball bounce off his head—
And hours later, I heard you were dead.

That evening, my two brothers were out at the game,
The Yankees played on, unknowing the name
That would echo through our home that night—
"Your father is gone." Just like that. No fight.

My brothers didn't hear it till the night was done,
But I was the first to learn that we were fatherless sons.
And I still remember what my brother said—
Our youngest cried at the game, tears he shed.

Couldn't explain it, didn't know why,
But maybe deep down, he felt the goodbye.
Children can sense what the heart can't define—
A soul on its way to crossing that line.

And still I wonder… **was he ever mine?**

I've heard some say you had good ways too—
You could cook, you could bake, you had rhythm in you.
You could drive anything that ran on wheels,
And you sang with a voice the heart could feel.

You loved the game—baseball, the craft,
But it was Ma who taught me how to track a bat's path.
You were a singer, but her voice raised me.
She gave me the soundtrack that made me, me.

You were a baker, but she taught me to stir,
To season with soul and to move like her.
You could drive anything on wheels, but she gave me drive—
The will to push through and come out alive.

So yeah, I got your gifts, I don't deny that,
But it was Ma who showed me where they sat.
She lit them up, made them real, made them mine,
Gave them to me in struggle and time.

Ma, I miss you dearly—every single day,
Your strength, your spirit, your nurturing way.
But you, Dad… I don't really miss you the same,
And it's not out of anger, or holding blame.

Maybe it's time, maybe it's truth,
Maybe it's growing up without you in youth.
But part of me does miss what I never had—
Not the man, but the chance of a loving dad.

A seat at the game, a picture three-fold—
You, me, my daughters—all stories told.
Advice on love, or even fixing a door,
Stories of you I could pass down and more.

Because now, I'm a father—twice through the gate,
With daughters 25 and 6, and for me this is great.

I was a young dad, now I'm an older one and more wise,
Seen both ends of life through a child's eyes.

And there's no greater thing I've ever done
Than to father my daughters, to raise them each one.
No title, no check, no victory high
Compares to the feeling of watching them try.

So help me understand, how could one deny
Their own flesh and blood, let that bond pass by?
I can't make sense of how one walks away
From something that lights your soul each day.

But most of all, I wonder this,
Now that you're both beyond the mist:
Have you seen her, have you two met?
Do you talk in peace, with no regret?

Do you sit side by side with the Most High near,
Able to speak without venom or fear?
Did she ask you the things that lingered in pain—
Like where were you through the hunger and rain?

Did she ask why her love turned to ash?
Why you left her with bills and no sort of cash?
Why the weight of the world fell on her back
While you watched from a distance, never picking up slack?

Did you tell her your fears, your doubts, your scars?
Did you both finally see each other for who you are?

And Ma—do you see him now, up there?
Do y'all even talk? Can you finally share

A moment without rage, without slamming doors,
Without "*YOU BLACK BASTARD*" echoing through the 8th floor?

You both had fire, but burned each other raw—
Now I pray that Heaven has a different law.

I recall you talking once, outside in the heat—
No yelling, no slurs, just talk on the street.

I couldn't hear what was said that day,
But I'll never forget that calm display.
Maybe that was a glimpse of what could have been,
If wounds weren't raw, and love had been thin.

So if you're both there, healed and free,
I pray you're talking, maybe even about me.
Because I carry the weight, the wonder, the cost,
Of the love that was broken, the time that was lost.

And Dad, if you hear me, I want you to know—
I don't hate you, I've just grown slow.
Slow to understand, but I'm getting there,
Unraveling truths in memory's stare.

I just wonder if you and Mom are civil enough to talk,
Now that she lived to be older than you did—
She made it to 80,
While you passed on before that milestone,
Leaving questions and regrets still unknown.

Is she wiser than you now, or is she still much younger?
Cause her life and experience have now surpassed yours,
Just something I wonder

Ma, save me a place in the front of your choir,
Where your voice still ignites,
Lighting that beautiful fire.
And Jimmy—if you've changed, then meet me there too,
In peace, in truth, in something new.

This is my truth, my heart laid bare—
Just your son, wondering, **now that you're both there.**

Double Edged

They say feminism was born with fire —
But whose flames lit the match?
When suffrage sang in satin gloves,
Black women still cleaned the ash.

They marched too, in borrowed shoes,
Past burning crosses and broken rules.
Fighting for rights they never abused,
Told to wait their turn — again — like fools.

The signs read *Votes for Women!* bold,
But whispered, *Just not you.*
Their wombs were fields, their backs were roads,
Their labor built the avenue.

Feminism had a front row seat,
But they were seated in the back.
They spoke of smashing glass ceilings
While she was dodging ceiling cracks.

She fought Jim Crow with lipstick on,
Braided protest in her hair,
She raised a nation in her arms
While the world pretended not to care.

Black men caught in the crosshairs,
Black women caught in between —
Told to choose: their race or gender,
When they bleed from both unseen.

But she ain't a victim. She's an architect.
Of movements, minds, and soul.

She loved us through the shackles,
Still climbed toward the goal.

She's not your angry trope or mule,
Not your Jezebel or Mammy.
She's complex, cosmic, unrefined—
A force too fierce for category.

So no, she don't need to be saved,
Just heard. Just held. Just free.
She ain't at war with brothers —
Just begging us to see.

See the layered load she carries,
The wisdom in her scars.
She ain't against us, beloved—
She just wants us all to go far.

So don't confuse her silence with surrender.
Don't mistake her strength for stone.
She's been bending backward for centuries—
Don't ask her to break alone.

It's not that she's too much.
It's that this world been too little.
She's the unsolved equation—
Y'all still stuck in the riddle.

And if she rolls her eyes at your ego—
That's just her lashes clapping back.

'Cause she been Black girl magic since before
Y'all even learned to say "Black."

So put some reparations in that respect.
Put some equity in that praise.
Don't crown her queen if you flinch when she rules—
That ain't love, that's just performative phase.

She don't need your permission to rise.
She BEEN sky. BEEN storm. BEEN flame.
And if you ever forget who taught you power—
Say her name. *Say her name.*

I come from questions, from love, from ache— but always from women who endured

Motivational Harassment

~A class E felony

For my friend Storm

It's a Class E felony—
E for Encouragement, not Escapism.
I've been booked and fingerprinted
For constantly reminding you
That greatness don't belong behind bars.

This ain't stalking, it's purpose-driven pursuit.
I'm guilty of motivational harassment—
Caught loitering around your potential,
Trespassing in your insecurities,
Soliciting your inner shine
Without a license.

Your gift been locked up too long,
Serving a life sentence in solitary doubt,
And I'm here filing motions for parole
On behalf of the dreams you keep ignoring.

You say, "I'm not ready."
I say, "That ain't up to you."
I'll be the loud cellmate of your silence,
Banging on the bars
Until your talent stands trial
And finally confesses to the world.

Call it reverse incarceration—
Un-incarcerated ambition,
Liberated light.
I'm the warden of your greatness,
But baby, I'm also the key.

I'll write you up for hiding your voice.
Cite you for resisting applause.
Violate your probation
Every time you minimize your magic.

This ain't soft love.
This is pep talk parole
With ankle monitor persistence.

I'm on your case like a lawyer with no chill,
Screaming "Objection!"
Every time you plead small.

You don't need bail—
You need belief.
And I'm posting both
Until your gift walks free
Without shackles,
Without shame,
Beyond all reasonable self-doubt—
The inmate of your brilliance
Finally getting out.

Garden of Dreams

In the darkest moments, when the night seems endless, there is still hope.
She carries it within her, a quiet flame that refuses to be extinguished.
Even as she shields her children from the storm, taking on the bruises so they don't have to,
she shows a strength that is both gentle and fierce.

She moves forward with courage, protecting her little ones,
making sure they know that even in the darkest times, they are loved and safe.
Her bravery is quiet but powerful, and it lights the way,
showing that even in the darkness, there is always a path forward.

In her mind, there is a garden of dreams,
a place where hope blossoms even in the shadiest areas of life.
She finds refuge there, a sanctuary where the chaos of reality softens into gentle whispers.
Her strength is in her ability to create this haven not just for herself,
but for her children, who remain blissfully unaware of the storms outside.
She transforms fear into stories of adventure,
loud noises into imaginary games,
and uncertainty into a journey towards something beautiful.
Even as she navigates her own fears,
she shows a bravery that is both quiet and profound,
ensuring that her children see only the beauty of the journey, not the dangers left behind.

In this garden of dreams, she nurtures hope,
and in doing so, she reveals the incredible strength of her spirit.

To anyone out there weathering storms—
Remember

Even when excuses and fears cloud the mind,
Know that strength and courage aren't hard to find.
If you feel there's nowhere to go, no one to turn to,
Remember that I stand with you, a friend to see you through.

The road ahead may have its twists and bends,
But keep moving forward; you don't need to make amends
For someone else's choice to cause you pain,
You are not alone, and your strength will remain.

And as the music softens, I lean in close,
This part is just for you, this is where I boast:
You have the courage, the strength to carry on,
Like a gentle lullaby, guiding you to dawn.

When the road is rough and the night feels long,
Remember that you're never truly alone.
You can rest here, safe in the knowledge that you're loved,
And that there's always hope, a light shining above.

So lift your head, look into my eyes,
Know that you are worthy, that you will rise.
And as the melody fades into the night so deep,
Know that you are safe, and tonight you can sleep.

Hopeful Flicker,
Leave the Light On

I waited with my coat on 'til the sky forgot the sun,
'Cause he said "after work," and maybe he meant "when I'm done."
Maybe the train broke. Maybe he got lost.
Maybe love gets stuck, but it ain't love's fault.

It's that flicker we keep—just a little light,
In the chest of a child on the third missed night.
By the door, by the phone, on a birthday cake—
That little flame that won't forsake.

It lives in the foster kid folding her socks,
Believing her mother will knock.
New rehab, new round, new chance to be clean,
She prays this time won't end like routine.

It's the boy whose dad said next weekend again,
So he draws superheroes with five o'clock shadow pens.
Still packs a bag, still ties his shoes,
Still checks the window for yesterday's news.

It's the wife who sets the table for two,
Even though she knows what he tends to do.
She believes in the vow more than he believes in himself—
Keeps hope on the top kitchen shelf.

It's the husband who waits at the edge of her phone,
Still believing love won't leave him alone.
She says she's tired, says "maybe later,"
But warmth turns cold, and touch turns vapor.
He kisses her cheek like it still means home,
While sleeping beside someone who's already gone.

It's the friend from the sandbox, thirty years strong,
But strong don't mean right, and right don't mean long.
They call when they're down, when they're broke, when they're low,
Say "I got you back," but they never show.
You loan the money, you share the ride,
Still hoping one day they'll stand by your side.
'Cause deep in your chest, that flicker still glows—
That maybe they mean it this time, who knows?

And it ain't weakness—it's grace,
To hope in the face
Of delay after lie after silence after stall—
To still believe someone might answer that call.

It's not denial—it's soul.
It's faith filling the hole.
A flicker that feeds the ones left waiting,
Still loving, still standing, still cultivating.

So light the porch lamp.
Keep the picture in the frame.
Somewhere in the ache of maybe
There's a strength that has no name.

The Only Thing to Fear Is...

What's in front of you?
A shadow?
A locked door?
Another boardroom you don't belong in?
Another badge that sees your skin before your soul?

You flinch.
Because you've been taught that fear is wise.
That looking over your shoulder keeps you alive.
That shrinking is surviving.
That silence is safer.
That invisibility is power.

But let's lay it bare.

Fear of being broken—
But weren't you already?
Didn't you survive the kind of heartbreak that tried to rename you?
Didn't you rebuild from fists, silence, gaslight, and guilt?

Fear of being hungry—
But didn't your stomach already echo like a choir of ghosts?
Didn't you stretch meals, ration dignity, and still serve someone else a plate?

Fear of being denied—
But weren't you born behind doors that slammed before you ever knocked?
Weren't you told "No" before your mouth could form "Why not?"

Fear of being poor—
But didn't you wear secondhand joy like it was couture?
Didn't you rock shoes with talking soles,
and still walk like a runway model through the hood?

Fear of being unwanted—
But didn't love abandon you in cribs, in classrooms, in courts?
Didn't you raise yourself in places that never asked your name?

Fear of racism—
But hasn't it always been here?
In boardrooms and breakrooms,
In hospitals and handcuffs,
In traffic stops and textbook lies?

Fear of falling—
But haven't you fallen already?
From jobs, from grace, from balconies of hope—
and still got up like gravity owed you money?

So tell me,
What haven't you faced?

You've survived the unthinkable and the everyday.
You've endured trauma in surround sound.
You've eaten disappointment for breakfast
and still smiled at your children like the world was good.

You have been brave when bravery wasn't even an option.
You were never taught how to swim—
yet here you are,
walking on water.

So what is there to fear?
Not the past.
You've outlived it.
Not the future.
You've earned it.

The only thing to fear is…
Nothing.

Because you are the storm.
You are the proof.
You are the legacy they tried to erase and failed to forget.

You are the child of fire and backbone,
a survivor with no scars visible enough to explain your strength.
And still—
you show up.
You rise up.
You look up.
You love again.

Bravery didn't knock.
You became it.

So hold your head.
Walk through every threat like it's déjà vu.
Because it is.

And you've already made it through.

Sometimes the truest sorry

comes from someone else's mouth

about something

you did to yourself.

—Freezy the Barber

Mrs. Hamer

Ancestral thunder, faceless, but never forgotten.
Her tears streaming cream—grief turned fertile,
Birthing life in one hand,
Balancing the world in the other.

No gold crown,
Just dread-forged fire
And a heart that pulses through hurricanes.
She does not weather the storm—
She **is** the storm.
A mother. A reckoning.
A vessel of pain and power,
Rising from the chaos
To cradle tomorrow.

Author's Note:

She mothered a movement.
She birthed the revolution in a rigged delivery room.
Fannie Lou Hamer was **forcibly sterilized without consent**—
Yet still became a maternal force through grit, justice, and voice.
She gave life to liberation, raised the volume of the unheard,
And held a nation accountable—not with violence, but with vision.
This poem honors not only her suffering,
But the unstoppable storm she became.

Vocally Shackled

They told her,
Speak your mind —
then stitched her lips with thread made of "calm down,"
pinned her tone to the floor
like a shadow that couldn't rise without shame.

They gave her a mic
but wired it to silence.
Let her scream
through a filter labeled angry,
then blamed the static
on her attitude.

Her voice was a freedom song —
but they redacted the verses,
looped the hook,
and sold it back to her
in a language she never sang.

She carried conversations
like cuffs,
measured each word
like contraband in the throat.
To be loud was to be labeled.
To be labeled was to be caged.

But every shackle rusts,
and every gag unglues.
When the echo finds its echo —
when the hush becomes a howl —
when the "too loud"
becomes the anthem…

She will speak.
Not for permission.
But for power.

Big Black Titties

Swollen with a world's need,
Marked for service, but never for freedom,
Bound to nourish, yet left to bleed,
A life of giving—who stops to feed them?

Once, they stood by cribs not their own,
Milk flowing, but never homegrown,
Their own flesh hungry, yet cast aside,
While white mouths latched, satisfied.

Big Black Titties, white only, they said,
Not fit for the water fountain,
But perfect to keep their babies fed.
A body treasured, yet never crowned,
Held up the world but never held down.

Still, they come—
To drink her dry, to take her strength,
To lean on her back 'til it breaks at length,
To set laws against her womb and fate,
To widen the gap, to make her wait.

Big Black Titties

She fights through cancer, through wage and womb,
Through hands that grab and systems that loom,
Through whispers that say she is too much, too loud,
Yet not enough to make them proud.

Degrees in hand, yet doors stay closed,
The most educated, yet under-chose.

They want her wisdom, her skill, her grace,
But not her voice, not her place. Paid less, but asked for more,
She carries the weight, the struggle, and the war.

Big Black Titties

No promotion, no fair pay,
Still, they need her every day.
To lead the work, to fix the mess,
To hold the home, to clean the stress.
And when the sickness comes to claim,
When the knife cuts deep and changes her name,
When the breasts that fed the world are gone,
Still—she nurtures, still—she holds on.

No longer able to nourish, yet never less,
Her love still lingers, her touch still blessed
For even without, she still provides,
Still feeds the world, still heals, still guides.

Big Black Titties, sacred, vast,
Will feed us all until the last.

Thank you.

Whoopi

They told us Celie was ugly—
said her skin was too deep, her braids too tight,
her smile too wide, her joy too bold,
but we know better now, don't we?

Entire aura, rich as the soil our roots grow from,
glowing like gold, braided like history,
cheeks full as laughter that won't be contained,
skin radiant like the sun kissing the dawn,
shining despite all they tried to dim.

Now we all know she's a Karen… individual,
lifting up children, standing for rights,
giving voice to the unheard, light to the fight.
A UNICEF warrior, a giver, a guide—
not just a star, but a force worldwide.

They tried to teach us that our coils were shame,
that our twists and "Whoopi braids" were chains,
but now we rock 'em like it's 1984,
like Celie never cried, like our "View" was never blurred,
like we been knew Whoopi was never ugly.

No eyebrows? No problem.
Who need 'em when your face is a masterpiece?
A Sistah Act so divine,
we see how real Sistas act—
bold, brilliant, brazen with beauty that they tried to erase but couldn't.

I will follow her,
like a choir in full harmony,
rockin' our twists, our coils, our locs,

loving the skin they told us to hide.
She led the song, and now we sing—
no shame, no fear, just beauty untamed.

From Celie to Sarafina,
Whoopi been leading, been teaching,
been showing us how to wear our truth,
how to grin in the face of lies,
how to laugh so loud it becomes legend.

Sister Mary Clarence? Nah, give her clearance!
Make way, roll out the purple carpet,
hand Whoopi her flowers—long overdue,
Oh and don't forget to give Celie
give Celie hers too.

Whoopi was never ugly.
That's only what we were told.
But now we know—
Whoopi was always gold.

Bald Head Baby Mama

My baby mama she ain't got no hair,
Smooth as the moon, rich melanin bare.
Not a curl, not a coil, not a twist in sight,
Still, she walks like a queen draped in golden light.

She don't need bundles, no wigs, no lace,
She wears her own crown with effortless grace.
She oils her scalp with all them ancient blends,
Says, "These roots run deep, they don't need no ends."

Her beauty ain't tied to no perm or press,
She's fierce in a sundress, bold in a vest.
With cowrie shells and wrists of gold,
She moves like a story that's never been told.

She is the storm, she is the calm,
Soft as shea, strong as psalm.
A Nubian empress, no need for disguise,
With wisdom so deep in those onyx eyes.

She sings to the spirits, she hums to the trees,
Burns sage in the morning, speaks love in the breeze.
She walks through the world like the Earth is her throne,
A goddess, a warrior, a force of her own.

People whisper, and some of em' stare,
"How she so fine with no hair up there?"
But she just laughs, "ha" she lets 'em be,
Says, "Beauty ain't scalp-deep, baby, it's in me."

And me? I'm lost, can't even pretend,
I fell in love once, then I fell again.

She had my back, she gave me peace,
She gave me life, my heart's release.

But here's the twist, don't blink, don't trip—
My bald head baby mama… stole my chick.

Ain't this a bitch?

…bald headed ass

Magic Rays of Sunshine

Sunlight dances across her curves, gliding over ridges
like golden trails in softened earth—raised, but never broken.
She's grown through storms—
not just rain, but hurricanes and heartbreak, tornadoes and time.
From earthquakes to contractions, she never cracked.
Still rooted, still rising.

Her body,
a land that birthed legacy, propagated power,
nurtured nations in her womb.
Her skin holds stories etched by time and transformation,
by the swell of creation and the ache of rebirth.
Brown like fertile earth, her skin absorbs the light,
reflects it back in silken ridges of resilience.

They call them scars—
I call them scripture.
Written in gold by the sun on the flesh of the divine.
Magic rays of sunshine,
blessing a body
that gave life and never asked for praise.

She Is a Woman

We call a female horse a mare and a female cow a cow. So why reduce a woman to just "female"? **Don't call her "female"**—that's calling her out of her name. Call her a woman, call her a lady, and honor who she is.

The Other Side of Strong

They called her strong because she never cried.
I called her strong because she finally did.

Butterfly Kisses

In the flutter of your lashes, I find a gentle breeze,
A whisper of affection that puts my heart at ease.
Your eyes, they speak in volumes, a language all their own,
And every blink, a butterfly, in a garden overgrown.

You melt beneath my gaze, a soft and tender glow,
A blush that speaks of butterflies, in ways only we know.
And in that gentle flutter, there's a message sweet and true,
That even as I look at you, I'm feeling butterflies too.

Let her be the center. I'll orbit gladly.

Wangari

Her skin, a canvas of rich, dark hues,
A story written in chocolate tones,
Eyes that carry the depth of worlds unseen,
Beautiful, wise, and endlessly warm.

Soft yet strong, like whispered strength,
A calm presence, an anchor in storms.

Her hands, like an artist's, weave memories,
Crocheting threads of comfort, like my mother's love reborn.

Her scars, etched maps of battles won,
Make her more radiant, a warrior unmatched.
Locks cascade, natural and proud,
A crown she wears, unbowed, unbroken…She's unbroken.

Wangari—her name, a melody sung,
Her movements, poetry crafted by time.
Fists that shield, kicks that strike,
A dance of power, grace in every line.

I'd kneel to kiss the very feet
That unleash those mighty, powerful kicks.
Strength and elegance in every blow,
She moves like a force the world should know.

If ever we collaborate on a legacy,
I hope they're built from 51 percent of her,
That her strength, wisdom, and beauty shine through,
And I'll proudly be the 49.

Though young, she carries centuries in her soul,
The masterpiece of a patient creation.
They started her long ago but took their time,
Perfecting each detail, every fiber divine.

She's the poem of centuries, perfected and whole,
And I'm the humble verse standing by her side.
A gift, a muse, a dream come true,
Wangari—she's mine, and I'm hers too.
Wangari—my stanza, poetry in motion.

Affirmation of Admiration

~Don't Mind Me

Don't mind me,
I'm just taking notes,
Tracing your beauty in rhythmic strokes.
That deep brown skin, like earth so pure,
Like autumn leaves in hues that lure.

Your cognac eyes hold untold tales,
A warmth that soothes, a light that sails.
They sip my soul with every glance,
A silent song, a whispered dance.

Don't mind me, had to pause a while,
To take in your grace, your flawless style.
You move in whispers, yet all can hear,
A presence loud without the cheer.

Tall and regal, you stand with grace,
Command the room, yet never chase.
Like a lioness, fierce yet still,
Power in poise, strength in will.

Don't mind me, but you lead so true,
Not a boss—no, that's not you.
You lift, inspire, and pave the way,
By showing first, not just what you say.

Don't mind me, but your voice is gold,
Soft and sultry, rich and bold.
It wraps me warm, it soothes me deep,
Like my mother's songs that rocked my sleep.

Don't mind me baby, just sitting back,
Admiring all the things you lack—
Nothing. Not a flaw in sight,
You move in whispers, still shine so bright.

Not too little, not too much,
Every piece—a perfect touch.
Style so bold, yet never confined,
Your presence lingers, undefined.

People love you, and I see why,
Your heart is pure, your soul won't lie.
You lift them up, you build me too,
A world is better just from you.

Don't mind me baby, but let's be clear,
Your assets? Baby, they're premier.
Yet in my world, they fit just right,
Like moonlit waves on velvet night.

Don't mind me, but I must confess,
You took my heart with no duress.
You claimed it long before you'd known,
Now all I want is to call you home.

Don't mind me baby, I'll take my time,
Drunk off love like sweet red wine.
Just one more look, just one more view,
Don't mind me—**I'm lost in you.**

Diasporic Love,

~A Trip Around Her World

She moves like the ocean, shifting with tides,
A rhythm-born goddess where history resides.
A melody humming in maroon-colored tones,
She speaks in a chorus of ancestors' bones.

From the shores of Accra to Nassau's embrace,
She carries the sun in the curve of her face.
A smile like Yemaya, wide as the sea,
She whispers in Creole, in Twi, in Patois to me.

In her skin, deep as cocoa, mahogany-bright,
Is the story of kingdoms lost to the night.
She oils her melanin, shea butter divine,
Her scent is of sandalwood, oud, and red wine.

She walks like a warrior, hips telling tales,
Of queens who once ruled and sisters in jails.
The strength of the Sotho, thick in her frame,
A blessing, a burden, a love with no shame.

Her hands braid revolutions, her locs touch the sky,
A halo of coils where spirits reside.
Crowned like Oshun, fierce as a storm,
She dances like thunder, relentless and warm.

The gospel of Harlem, the blues of the South,
The jazz in her laughter, the heat in her mouth.
Salsa in The Bronx, zouk from Cayenne,
Reggae and dancehall, she sings them again.

Her voice is a sermon, her body a shrine,
She prays in mosques and temples divine.

She kneels in the pews, she burns sacred sage,
Holding the prayers of a world in her gaze.

From Joberg to Kingston, Nairobi to Queens,
Her footsteps awaken ancestral dreams.
She builds, she births, she bends but won't break,
She is the drum of the earth, the sound, the quake.

Diasporic love, a lesson, a flight,
Through time and through culture, through day and through night.
She carries the world in the sway of her hips,
A passport of passion, a journey in her lips.

And as I move closer, she remakes my soul,
Teaching me stories my bloodline should know.
For loving her—this woman, this world—
Is loving myself, my past, my pearls.

She is the continent, the islands, the moon and the stars,
A map of survival, of healing, of scars.
A love that will travel, reshape and expand—
For she is the ocean, and I am her land.

I Touched Her with My Mind First

Before my hand ever brushed her skin,
my mind was already tracing the lines of her thoughts,
following the curves of her imagination,
finding beauty in the way she sees the world.

Our conversations were like poetry,
words dancing and weaving tapestries of meaning,
each sentence a brushstroke on the canvas of our connection.

In the silence between our voices,
there was a resonance, a knowing,
a touch that needed no physical form to be felt.

They connected in thought
before they ever touched.
But when they did—
it told the truth they couldn't say out loud.

Soft Places, Hard Truths

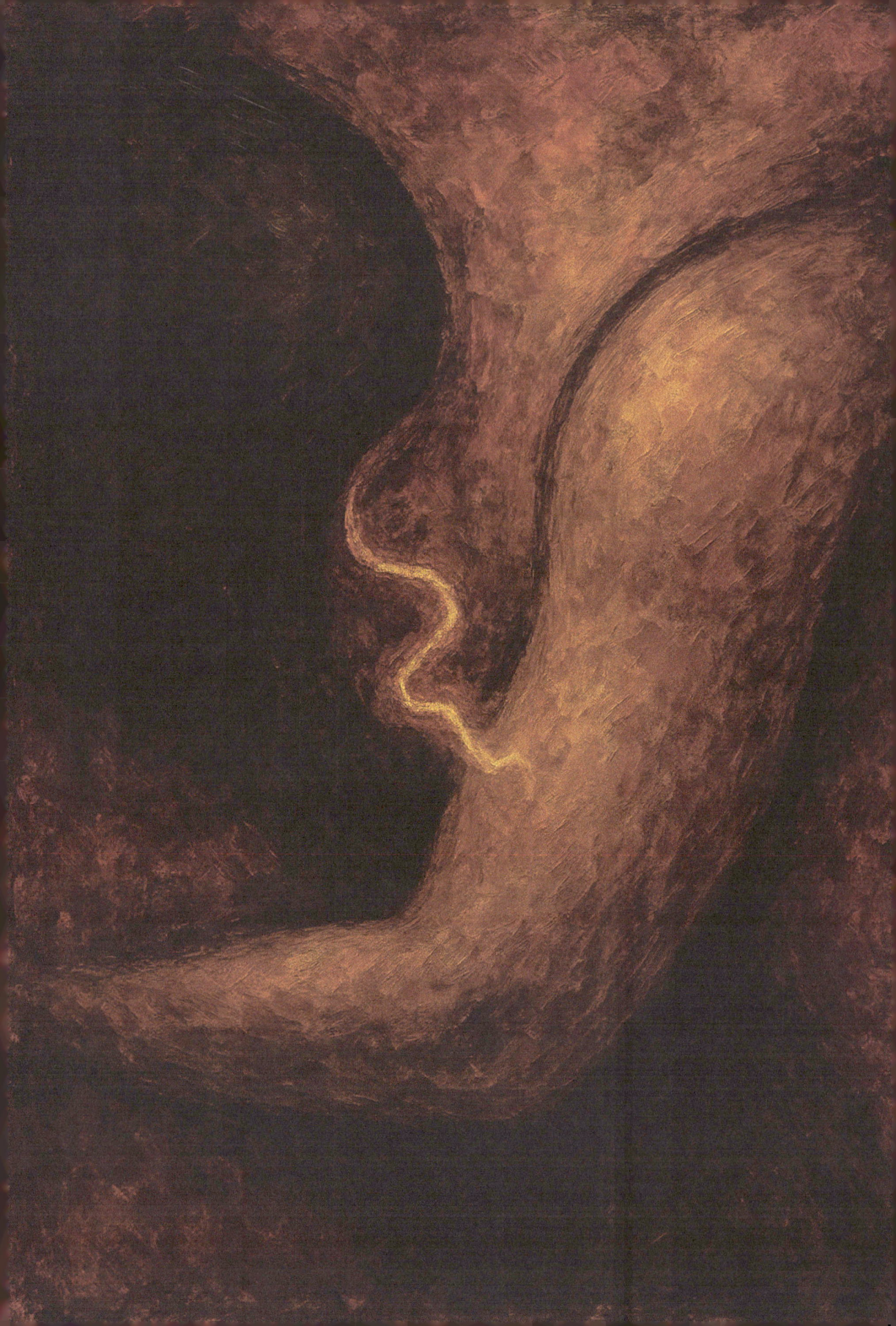

There are places on her body
where my hands stop speaking
and just listen.

Where softness dares me to be still,
to feel
without needing to fix.

Thigh, belly, nape—
mapped in melanin and memory.
Not just skin,
but sanctuary.

And in those folds,
between sighs and stares,
I hear the truth louder
than any "I love you" whispered too soon.

She moans without permission—
not just from pleasure,
but from recognition.

I feel her saying:
You can't enter here without consequence.
You can't touch this and pretend it meant nothing.
This is where softness
holds court.

Where the body cries out
what the mouth won't admit—
that something real is growing,
right here,
in sweat and silence.

And the hard truth is:
we may call it casual,
but these hips remember.
This connection convicts.

Black love don't stay surface.
It roots.
It pulls.
It knows.

Even in the dark,
we leave fingerprints on each other's soul.

This isn't lust pretending to be love—
this is something older.
An echo passed down from porch swings
and midnight hushes.
From slow-dancing in basements
to hush-your-mouth glances at family cookouts.

We speak in rhythms.
In shifts of breath.
In the hush before a name is gasped.

And somewhere between her back arching
and my chest breaking open, we learn: pleasure doesn't lie—
but it does tell the truth we've been ducking.

That this matters.
That we matter.

That soft places
can house hard truths like:
"I see you,"
"I need you,"
"I'm not going anywhere."

And when the bodies settle,
and the sweat turns cool,
and silence reclaims the room—
what remains
is stillness.

Not empty,
but full.

A quiet knowing
only we can name.
Where nothing else moves,
but everything feels understood.

After the truth is spoken in touch,
the body starts to sing.

Where the Bassline Lives

In the rhythm of our connection,
there's a pulse, a deep hum that resonates beneath the surface,
like the steady thump of a bass drum,
each beat a whispered promise, a lullaby in the quiet afterglow.

Where the bassline lives,
our bodies speak a language of their own,
the soft clap of skin meeting skin, a percussive symphony of closeness,
a rhythm that echoes in the space between heartbeats.

In the curve of her form, in the arch of the moment,
the sound we create is a song we both know by heart,
a melody that draws us closer,
each note, a testament to the harmony we share.

And when the world quiets,
and she rests her head against my chest,
she hears that deep, thunderous melody within,
a comforting cadence of me speaking about my dreams that lulls her into
her dreams.

It's in this harmony of sound and sensation,
where words fade and feeling takes over,
that we find a place of pure connection,
where the bassline of our love plays on.

These aren't perfect truths. They're just truths.

Oxymoronic Love

She is my joy that causes so much pain,
My sun that brings the endless rain.
The warmth that chills me to the bone,
The place I crave, yet feel alone.

She's the laughter tangled with my tears,
The calming voice that stirs my fears.
The one I know, for whom I fall,
The one I wish I'd never known at all.

She's the opposite of all I need,
In fact she's my heart's own creed.
A paradox, a cruel delight,
My shadowed day, my blinding night.

The celebratory thing I grieve
She's every wound I can't relieve.
So obviously subliminal,
My law-abiding criminal.

She's the giver of life that steals my soul,
My half that never makes me whole.

The breath of fresh air
That takes my breath away
The unfulfilling satisfaction
Of an accelerated delay

She's everything wrong, with everything that's right,
The storm I love, my favored plight.

Cozy is where my feelings go when they're too tired to stand.
Where I can speak freely without editing my soul.
It's the soft space in your presence that tells me,
"This is not a courtroom. This is not a stage. This is home."

Cozy is when I rest my head on you
And the noise of the world hushes like a child at bedtime.
Where silence doesn't mean distance —
It means peace.
It means safety.

It's not just warmth — it's trust with a blanket on.
It's knowing I can hand you the tender, trembling parts of me
And you won't try to fix them or expose them —
You'll just hold them.

Cozy is where secrets go to be soothed,
Where feelings are folded, not thrown.
It's where I can say,
"I'm not okay,"
And you won't flinch.

You'll just be there.
Like the therapist I never had,
But more —
Because you love me through it.
Because we don't need credentials
understand each other.

You're my cozy.
My lockbox.
My exhale.
My sanctuary with arms.

Pheromone

She ovulates like the moon commands tides—
a silent pull I can't deny.
Skin glowing like Yemaya's blessing,
hips humming with ancient pride.

The air thickens
not with perfume,
but with pheromones and purpose.
She don't wear fragrance,
she *is* the fragrance—
sweet and warm like shea on skin,
thick, creamy,
like the first pour of raw honey
from a Black grandmother's jar.

My beard twitches at the scent—
magnetic,
as if follicles know
what science already said:
She's ripe.
And I'm right
where I'm supposed to be.

I approach not as predator,
but as priest.
Each follicle on my face a whisper,
each breath a sermon.
She parts the veil with a look—
says nothing,
but my ancestors nod from the dust.

"You attract me," I murmur,
as if it's a choice.

But nature done chose for me.
Your body's signal—a flame.
My biology responds—
a moth with rhythm.
Your thighs, a continent.
Your womb, a drumbeat.
I follow the beat.

Not just to lay with you—
but to align.
Because you're not just ovulating.
You're creating.
You're summoning the divine.
And I—I bring nothing less
than worship.

And when my hands find you,
they don't just touch—
they testify.
These are the hands that heal,
that fade men and fix things,
but were built
for the blessed softness
of you.

You say I got that magic grip—
that squeeze that melts you
every time.

Like your booty was clay
and I was born to sculpt it.
Like I was taught by gods
who loved roundness
and reverence.

Your skin—
rich like cocoa butter in summer heat,
velvet over power,
the perfect texture between my palms.
And when I press,
you sigh—
like your muscles remember
what they were made for.

But it's your center
that changes the rules.
That thick, creamy sweetness
you keep locked away
like a sacred offering—
baby, that ain't just desire.
That's alchemy.

When you bloom,
it's Cadbury in the sun—
soft shell giving way
to nectar and warmth.
Silky.
Velvety.
Tasting like the secret
of every fruit Eve was warned not to bite.

My beard gets baptized
in that holy cream,
and I don't rush—
nah.
I savor—Like I'm fasting
and finally allowed to feast.

Like every note of your body
deserves its own page in the Book of Psalms.

And the way you grab my wrist,
your hips arching—
you ain't just reacting.
You're composing.
You're the whole symphony.
And I—
I'm just the instrument
you chose to play.

This ain't lust.
This is lineage.
This is Harriet's fire,
Angela's spine,
a rhythm encoded in the genes
of women who made freedom feel
like home.
And now—
you're home.

We don't just make love.
We remember it.
We summon it
from beneath the floorboards of the ships

the hush of southern porches,
the sweat of sharecroppers
who still managed to kiss
under the stars.

We sweat in sync
like it's protest and praise.
My beard—wet with devotion.
Your thighs—trembling testimony.

And I would write scriptures
in every drop
if only I could catch them
before they bless my chest.

So ovulate, love.
Glow, shine, pulse.
Let your softness soften me.
Let your taste
teach me languages
I never knew I knew.

Because when your body calls,
mine don't just answer—
it kneels.
It gives thanks.
It remembers
that before there was science,
there was you.
There was this.
And there was us.

When touch fades,
intention becomes the only way to hold her.

Felt Without Touch

There are touches that never make contact.
Fingertips that never meet,
but still stir the skin.

Words can caress.
Voice notes can graze the neck If you close your eyes.
Laughter can press against your chest
like a hand you wish was there.

Some connections bloom in the absence of bodies.
The mind reaches first.
Then the spirit leans in.

We were a slow dance with no music.
A fire lit by eye contact on a screen.
A longing born not of flesh,
but of thought.
And still, somehow, it burned.

What we shared wasn't casual.
It was crafted.
Every text, every late-night call, every pause—
intentional.

It wasn't just affection—it was architecture.
We built this.
Carefully.
Deliberately.
Without touch.

But something about the space between us
made everything feel bigger.

Desire swelled,
but so did vision.

We dreamed louder from a distance.
Talked about things we might've whispered in person.
Planned freely,
loved hypothetically,
until our fantasies felt like facts
waiting for a date to show up.

You'd say,
"Imagine if we were in Ghana right now,"
and suddenly we were.
Sipping something sweet on a rooftop,
watching people dance.
We built whole worlds from pixels.

And the wild part?
It felt real.

We went everywhere together,
without moving an inch.
Because our minds were free.
Because our hearts were brave.
And if we can do all that in the not-yet,
what can't we do in the now?

Ours is not the first love to stretch across distance.
Ours is not the first to live in imagination
long before it ever touched ground.

There were men who counted the days
until they could sneak one more glance
at the woman picking okra across the fence line.

There were women who saved their softness
for moonlight,

when the overseers slept,
and whispers could turn to kisses in the dark.

Love letters weren't written—they were memorized.
Eyes became promises.
Time became prayer.

Black love has always made a way.
Across plantations.
Across front porches split by county lines.
Across years of being told we couldn't choose,
couldn't keep,
couldn't build.

Even now,
something is always trying to keep us apart.
But we still dream.
Still project.
Still plan.
Still reach.

Because this kind of love?
It doesn't just survive the distance.
It defines it.

People say long-distance relationships never last.
And maybe they're right.
But that's the thing—
they're not supposed to last.
They're meant to lead.

Lead into presence.
Into intention.
Into the warmth of arms that don't glitch or buffer.

They're meant to lead into waking up beside
the mind that kept you up all night.
To cooking meals with the hands you once imagined.
To real arguments, not delayed responses.
To kisses that don't depend on imagination.

This—
this isn't forever.
This is the proof of what could be,
a preview with soul.

And it takes intention.
Because love, at a distance,
requires planning.
Patience.
Faith in something you can't touch today,
but are building for tomorrow.

Black love like this doesn't float—it fights gravity.
It demands to land.

To root.
To grow in real soil, not just signals

It's not meant to last this way.
It's meant to become something greater.
And we—we are meant to arrive.

"Black Love
is a metaphysical response
to a world designed
to unmake it."
—Freezy the Barber

Lavender was my mother's
favorite color.
That's why I chose it for the
spine of this book. Because
she is the spine of my art.
She's where I got it from.

Manhood is not a destination. It is a quiet choice to show up when no one is watching, to break cycles without breaking yourself. --Freezy the Barber

No Asterisk,

~And It's Not Just About Cheesecake

A poem for Dominae

You said you didn't want it.
Just a slice. Just a taste.
"It's just cheesecake," you shrugged.
But baby, it was never just that.

It was about saying yes to life.
To trying.
To trusting.
To stepping out the box they try to keep you in.

See, I've been fighting for you
since before you even knew what fighting looked like.
Not with fists,
but with presence—
with showing up when no one else would.

You came into this world at 7:17 p.m.,
April thirteenth, nineteen ninety-nine,
and I've been showing up ever since.
Your mama and I—
we weren't meant to last.
But you and me?
We were built to endure.

My family?
They don't even blink.
You're one of us.
No asterisk. No explanation.
You just are.

You moved like my mother,
talked like my sisters,
ate like you had little pinkies made of glass.

You were family,
not by blood,
but by breath, by being,
by the rhythm in your laugh
and the way you and Diamond's faces mirrored each other's,
like God said,
"Let me remind him this one's his."

They never asked questions
because they never needed to.
You were already woven in.

You grew up in the barbershop,
made a killing off cuss words—
every "damn" worth a dime,
every "shit" worth a quarter.
You were stacking coins
and catching wisdom between haircuts.

And still, I was working nights
at a pickle factory,
then cutting heads by day,
but always back in time
to walk you into school

and sit through morning lessons
like that was my paycheck.

Because it was.
You were.

You weren't an accident.
You weren't a burden.
You were the daughter
I always knew I'd have—
not given to me,

but chosen by me.
And I chose right.

But it wasn't always easy,
and love ain't always peaceful.

Sometimes,
I had to wrestle for the right to be your father—
not in courtrooms,
but in conversations that cut.
There were times
your mama would stir storms
just to watch the wind spin.
She told you at seven—
not with tenderness,
but with timing meant to sting—
that I wasn't your "real" dad.

As if love
ever needed a blood test.

You didn't flinch.
And neither did I.
Because you already knew the truth:
what's real
is who stays. And I stayed.

Even when I had nothing left
but a pair of pants
and pride stitched into every step.
Even when I was homeless
with a barbershop key in my pocket,
pretending everything was fine
so your world wouldn't crack.

I made sure your birthdays still lit the sky.
Especially that ninth one—remember that?
Hannah Montana blaring in a full-on nightclub,
strobe lights dancing like they were paid to.
Sixty, seventy kids wild on sugar and song,
half of them strangers
but all of them guests
at the party of the decade.
The bar shut down,
but the dance floor was wide open—
just like your smile.

You twirled through that club
like it was built just for you.
And maybe it was.

Because on that day,
the world paused
and said,
"Let her shine."

And let's not forget Deebo—
your favorite boy cousin,
thirty now but always that kid.

At your big party,
when the piñata finally gave in,
he dove like he'd been training for it,
stretched his whole body
across the floor like a linebacker in church socks,
and swept up seventy percent of the candy
before the others even blinked.

While the rest of the kids were locked
in a sugar-starved Royal Rumble
over what was left,
there he was—
cool as ever,
packing his bag,
one piece at a time,
not a care in the world.

That's the kind of day it was—
chaotic, magical,
yours.

Now she's twenty-six,
but I still call her my teenager.
We live under the same roof,
but sometimes it feels like
I need a permission slip just to knock.

She slips past me
like love might be contagious,
like my affection is too loud
for the cool she's trying to keep.

But I see her—
that little girl's still in there,
under the grown-up sighs
and closed bedroom doors.
Still my daddy's girl,
even if she's undercover about it now.

Truth is,
I made her a sore loser—
and I'll own that.

Every time she lost a guessing game,
she'd pout and cry,
and I'd slide her the money anyway.
Hell, sometimes more than the prize.
I'd be like,
"Here, baby—it's not just about winning."

Even though it was.
She wanted to win,
and I wanted her to never feel like she'd lost.

I spoiled her rotten—
like a peach in July.
Soft and sweet
and probably too protected.

Now I'm stricter with Journey,
laying down lines I used to erase for Dominae.
Funny how time makes you wise
and guilty all at once.

I'm learning balance from them both—
how to hold on and let go,
how to show up without showing out,
how to protect without smothering
and guide without gripping too tight.

Dominae taught me what it means to fight for love—
to choose it, claim it,
even when it's complicated,
even when the world says,
"you don't have to."

She made me softer
before I knew what soft could be—

she cracked open a part of me
that had never been used before.

Journey,
she's teaching me boundaries.
She's showing me that love
doesn't always mean saying yes,
that protection sometimes comes
in the form of structure,
that presence isn't just physical—
it's principled.

One made me a father.
The other made me better at it.

I look at them both
and see two different versions of grace:
one earned in the fire,
the other refined in the light.

And me?
I'm still learning.
Still adjusting the grip.
Still holding them both in my heart—
different hands,
same love.

I was a good dad
before it was cool.
Before "girl dads" were trending,
before TikTok made fatherhood a flex,
I was doing it for real.

No accidents.
No "oops" baby.
I made a choice—
to step in,
to stay in,
to stand in the gap.

And the same dudes who called me soft,
who laughed behind my back
like I was some simp-ass clown
for raising a child that wasn't "mine"…
meanwhile they weren't even watering their own seeds.

They're still out here
chasing weekends and wondering
why their kids don't even talk to them.

Meanwhile,
Dominae's been clocking in,
showing up,
handling life like she took notes
from the way I loved her.

She never missed school
those first few years in North Carolina.
Not once.
Not until Great-Grandma Nana passed—
and even then,
she checked out early,
paid her respects,
and still showed up to life.

That's what I raised—
a woman who shows up.

And it started with walking her to class,
cutting hair on no sleep,
putting my wants in my back pocket
so she could have a full childhood
without the burden of knowing
how broke her daddy was.

She don't carry shame.
She carries legacy.

So Dominae,
if you ever read this—
if you ever need to remember who you are
and how you got here—
just know this:

You were chosen.
You were fought for.
You were the first heart I gave away
without hesitation.

I might've spoiled you,
I might've enabled you a little too much,
but I did it because I saw your light
and wanted it to shine without struggle.

You changed me—
from a boy with clippers
to a man with purpose.
From someone searching
to someone steady.

And even now,
when you act like daddy's love

is a little too loud,
I still see that little girl in the club,
dancing under strobe lights,
watching Deebo hoard all the candy,
laughing like the world was hers.

It still is…
And so am I.

Always.

I raised a child before I finished being one.
But somehow, we both grew up
and met manhood in the middle.

Thought Bubble

We shared a thought bubble—
not a metaphor, a real one.
Like a comic strip hovering over three heads,
cartoon clouds connecting craniums,
every scene drawn from the same memory bank,
captioned in unison.

Me, Chink, and Josh—
three boys in a four-bedroom apartment
stuffed with twenty sum odd people
and enough love to expand the square footage.
The hallway barely wide enough for grown-man shoulders
was an entire stadium when we were small.
That place?
It wasn't just a home.
It was a whole damn world.

We played full-court basketball
in a hallway so tight,
now I gotta turn sideways just to pass through.
Wire hangers became hoops,
top of the door the backboard,
the floor our concrete parquet,
sneakers squeaking in our minds.

Our bedroom?
The Gladiator Arena.
Like American Gladiators on public housing floors.
We'd climb the closet like it was the Wall event,
wedge a jump rope with knots in the door
and scale it like it led to glory.
Top bunk dismantled,

dresser turned into a launchpad—
Macho Man elbows off the top rope
onto My Buddy dolls
in three-on-three tag team wars
like they were gunning for our belts.

We weren't just playing—
we were becoming.
Living the lives we dreamed up
on bunk beds and barbershop chairs.
Pretending to be grown—
with jobs, kids, responsibilities.
Chink always had a son named J-ski.
I always had a daughter.
And now?
Jacob is Jay-ski.
And I got my little girls.

That thought bubble wasn't just play—
it was prophecy.

Josh—Dirt—
we still talk in acronyms.
Whole sentences,
first letters only.
"W-Y-D-W-L-D-A"
And he knows.
Still.
That's not a language.
That's brotherhood.

We were raised by sisters,
shaped by their scars,

shielded by their strength.
They didn't just raise us—

they preserved us.
Their missteps warned us.
Their love guided us.

We stayed outta trouble.
Not because it didn't knock.
But because imagination always answered first.
While the streets were calling kids by name,
we were too busy
trying to win World Series replays in the hallway,
too deep into being Jordan and Drexler
to hear the block whisper.
And if someone knocked over mommy's fan,
game over.
But we'd reset.
Always.

Jamie teases us now.
Calls us "boy moms"
'cause we do the diapers,
braid the hair,
pack the snacks,
check the homework.
She jokes with our wives—
"Oh, he let you hold his daughter?"
Mocking our spouses as if they're lucky we let them parent.

But that's us.
Hands-on.
Hearts all in.

We're grown now.
Fathers.
Providers.
Still friends.

Still calling each other like,
"Ayo, what happened in '89?"
And without hesitation—
"You mean when Fred doodoo'd in the tub?"
Same memory.
Same laugh.
Same damn thought bubble.

We didn't make it to the majors.
Didn't sign to Motown.
Didn't hoist NBA trophies.
But we became
exactly who we imagined.
And that's the flex.

I wanted to be a barber—
been cutting since fourteen.
Still doing it, thirty years later.
Living the dream I whispered
in that little room

with wrestling belts made of cardboard
and clients made out of my sister's dolls.

We made it past forty.
We're still here.
When so many
from our block
ain't even make it to half that.

We're proof
that imagination can save you.
That love can raise you.
That three boys
in a cramped apartment

can build whole lives
out of hope and concrete floors.

If we weren't blood,
we'd still be chosen.
Still brothers.
Still in sync.

Different lives.
Same love.
Different homes.
Same damn comic strip
drawn across decades.
One giant bubble,
three boys still living inside it.

They mocked the vision because they never had one.

Heir of the Block

We grew up on the same streets,
same concrete under our feet,
But while you stayed rooted,
thinking the block was the peak,

I chose to climb,
to fight the cycles and temptations,
To be the tough guy
who toughs out poverty with aspirations.

You laughed at the dress shoes,
the interviews, the dreams,
While you stood in Jordans,
guarding the same old scenes.

I say making it in New York
means making it out,
To rise above the noise,
to stand out from the crowd.

I chose the tougher road,
built a life, a legacy,
While you hold up the same corners,
a cycle of complacency.

Here's to the real tough ones,
who fought to break free,
The true heirs of the block,
who choose their own legacy.

Go Ahead, Pick that Bear, Sis

The algorithm taught you that. Not the ancestors.

Let Him Be Heard

La la la…"—I hear it now,
A melody of disregard.
My lips move, yet you tune me out,
Like static noise, like passing cars.

I stand, a man—broad shoulders, firm,
A heart that beats but dares not bleed.
For every tear I might have shed
Has long since dried, dismissed as weak.

"Zesty." "Sassy."—words like chains,
Wrapped tight around my right to feel.
If I object, they call it rage,
If I submit, I'm not real steel.

Yet who stands firm when storms arise?
Who catches tears with steady chest?
Who carries burdens, never cries,
Yet always gives, yet never rests?

We die first. The records show.
More widows weep than widowers grieve.
For we hold in what needs to go,
Till breath is short and hearts deceive.

"La la la…"—you hum again,
A lullaby to hush my truth.
Do my words disturb your peace,
Or just the mirror they hand you?

I don't recall the last time pain
Flowed freely from these weary eyes.

I've held shit in so long, I think
I forgot how to cry.

But know this—when you collapse,
When sorrow makes you fold and break,
My chest will be your steady bass,
The rhythm that your soul can take.

All I ask—just hear me too.
Don't cut me down for knowing self.
My strength is not in caged-up wounds,
But wisdom that preserves my health.

"La la la…"—but not this time.
No muted ears, no sidelong glance.
Our pain, our plight should never fall
On deafened hearts, on empty hands.

Emotional intelligence is just that—intelligence.
The wisdom to know, the courage to speak,
The depth to feel, the strength to think,
To balance mind and soul, not sink.

It is not softness. It is not flaw.
It is not weakness wrapped in straw.
It is the reason I still stand,
The anchor, not just idle hands.

I'm not against you, we are one.
My frame is built to guard, protect,
But even warriors come undone
When all they give is no respect

So let me purge, let me release and let go,
And see my heart as not less man.
For what is intelligence but growth,
And what is strength but one who can?

You Don't Need the World to Tell You

Don't wait for the world to validate you.
Know you're worthy—
because someone who matters
already told you the truth.
 And if you ever forget it,
remember I said it first.
With no applause,
no cameras,
no crowd.
Just your daddy,
looking you in your eyes,
like you're the whole sun
and I'm just thankful to be warm.

You Good Bro?

In those quiet moments, when the world doesn't see,
There's a weight we carry, heavy as can be.
We stand as the pillars, always holding strong,
Expected to be the heroes, never to go wrong.

But who asks the question, "You good, bro?" with care,
When the burdens get heavy and the load's hard to bear?
We're more than just providers, fixers of things,
We feel, we hurt, we dream, we worry about things.

In a world that demands we stay stoic and strong,
We swallow our pain, we've done it for so long.
But strength isn't silence, and tears aren't weak,
Sometimes we just need a safe space to speak.

To be seen as a human, not just a role,
To share in the journey, to lighten the toll.
So, brother, I'm asking, with all that I know,
From one heart to another, truly:

You good, bro?

HANDS

Some build, some bruise, some forget they can do both.

Proud American,

~By virtue of nothing

I was ***born in the U.S.A.***—
Cue the fireworks and eagle screech, hooray!
A doctor spanked my butt in freedom's land,
So now I wave a flag with my burger-stained hand.

No passport needed to claim elite worth,
I earned it all… by simply showing up at birth.
No effort, no test, no global audition,
Just popped out crying into a top-tier position.

"Best country in the world!" we yell, loud and plucky,
While not knowing the world beyond Build-A-Bear Kentucky.
The map is just America, the rest? Who cares!

Africa's one big jungle with lions and "deers"—
I mean… gazelles. Whatever. Nobody really cares?

We picture kids in clay huts just swatting flies,
As if Wi-Fi and skyscrapers are Westernized lies.
"You're from Uganda? Wow, so brave!"
As if the Bronx ain't got potholes the size of a grave.

Meanwhile, little Timmy in Detroit eats chalk,
But we send 20 cents a day to help "African toddlers" walk.
A white savior ad plays—cue the sad violin—
While U.S. schools can't afford books or pens.

We think their trees are all banana and their cars are goats,
That every child drinks puddle water and dreams of our boats.
While in Lagos they code and dance to Afrobeats,
We're googling "Does Africa have concrete streets?"

Ethnocentrism: our national pastime,
Behind baseball and pretending racism's "just fine."

"Speak English!" we bark, with glorious pride,
While butchering GYROS and schnitzel worldwide.

We claim to be melting pot saints, born to lead,
But won't eat hummus 'cause it sounds "Middle East-y."
We demand allegiance from folks abroad,
As if "Proud American" is a gift from God.

Like every baby born in Arkansas
Should get a global round of applause.
"You're welcome," we say, without having helped,
As if we personally built the Liberty Bell.

But pride without merit is just a costume and song,
And nationalism blindfolds what's right and what's wrong.
So salute the flag, sure—but know what it's worth:
You didn't earn America. Your ass just fell to Earth.

Built on bones and stolen land,
Where genocide and slavery go hand in hand.
"Home of the brave" means "land of the thief,"
Where plantations grew cotton and systemic grief.

Funny how white folks are such a small slice—
Just over 800 million… ain't that nice?
Nearly half live right here, proud and loud,
Yelling "We built this!" from a blood-soaked cloud.

Meanwhile in India, a single nation,
Holds more people than white folks in the whole damn population.
Yet somehow, it's the pale ones who run the banks and bombs,
Must be that special brand of generational wrongs.

Could it be—just maybe, slight suggestion—
They're the only ones who ever needed world possession?
Greedy enough to trade gold for a cross,
Evil enough to call profit "manifest loss."

We forgive while they imprison, hug while they shoot,
We water dead flowers, they yank up the root.
They want the electric chair for a man who stole grapes,
While we're hugging our child's killer, and praying for their sake.

So next time you chant "USA, USA,"
Maybe pause and ask, "What price did we pay?"
Because being proud with no moral rebirth—
Isn't patriotism.
It's privilege by birth.

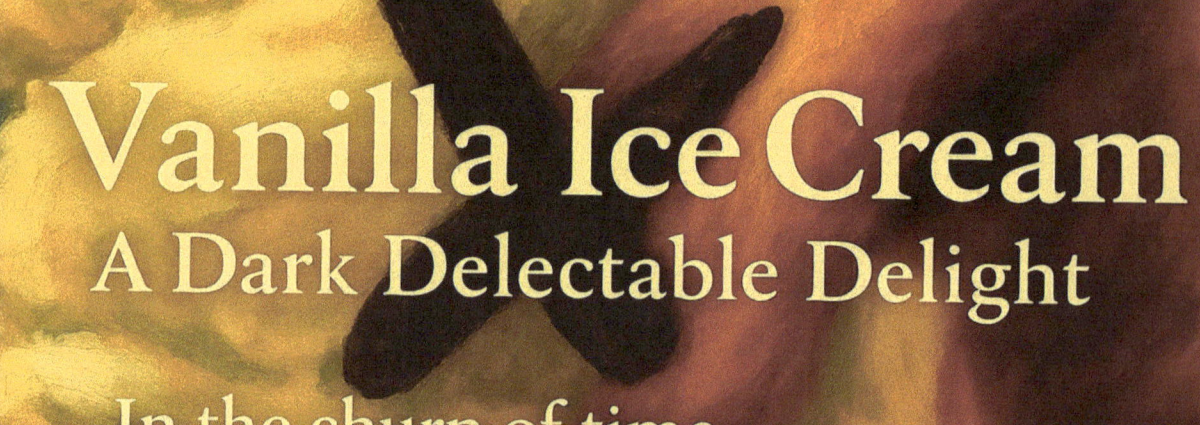

Vanilla Ice Cream
A Dark Delectable Delight

In the churn of time,
the purest hue they claim,
yet from the darkest bean,
the sweetest essence came.

Twice Oppressed

From the motherland we came, spirits unbroken, souls aflame,
Stripped of language, of culture, of name,
yet the magic in us remained the same.

We built new rhythms, carved out new songs,
Stacked our pain into pyramids where it still belongs.
From hush harbors to Harlem nights,
We birthed joy in the belly of stolen rights.

But when we reach back, fingers digging through soot and blood,
Hoping to trace our lineage beyond the flood—
We find pages burned, scrolls gone missing,
Names dissolved by history's selective kissing.

Not just by whip, but by ink we were denied—
Erased from records where others' truths reside.
Even well-meaning hands reframe the tale,
Softening truth for comfort's sale.

In the silence of the archives, in the ashes of what's left,
We are twice oppressed, even by those with the best intent.

Yet still, we rise, our legacy persists,
In every note of jazz, in every soulful twist.
Our story's not in their papers, but in the strength we possess,
Unbreakable, unyielding, despite being twice oppressed.

They say "we didn't know," but ignorance, too, oppresses—
It's the echo of silence when justice confesses.
Twice oppressed—first by force, then by forgetfulness,
Yet still, we press, dressed in ancestral finesse.

We are not your half-told stories or your tragic refrain—
We are griots in flesh, encoded with pain.
We are the legacy that leaps off the page—
The gospel, the hip-hop, the fire, the sage.

You won't find us in the footnotes of shame,
We've been authors of glory without needing acclaim.
Our history may not fill their shelves—
But we carry libraries within ourselves.

Twice oppressed, but never erased—
We rise through the smoke, with elegance and grace.
Rooted in truth they tried to suppress—
We bloom, we roar, we love—**regardless**.

I Said What I Said

Just because you said it, don't make it true,
Your world nods along, but only for you.

It's fine, it's okay, they all say with a smile,
Because it's your reflection they follow, mile after mile.

In the dance of words, the power's in the who,
For what's deemed right or wrong depends on the view.

Ironic Hilarity

They say beauty is in the eye of the beholder, but the irony's clear,

It's not the men holding the mirror, but the whispers we hear.
Dragged across screens, it's a tale as old as time,
Critiques from all sides, but who's really drawing the line?

They say we set the standards, but let's pause and reflect,
Is it really our gaze or the clicks and the effect?

The irony is rich, the hilarity bittersweet,
In a world of endless opinions, who's really in the driver's seat?

Why is Jesus So Mean?

They say I stray from the fold, a rogue in the night,
But I'm just seeking my truth, my own guiding light.
In the halls where the hymns rise, echoing strong,
They preach endurance, but I question the song.

"This life be over soon, heaven lasts always,"
Yet my sister's yearning was for earthly days.
She fought to breathe, to laugh, to thrive,
Why must she perish to feel alive?

To be a leader, they say, is to follow the creed,
To march to the drum of another man's need.
But I'm not a pawn in a sanctified game,
I forge my own path, I carry my name.

From the shadows of slavery, a tool to control,
Faith was wielded to shackle the body and soul.
We're told to obey, to follow the preacher's decree,
But what of the freedom to simply be me?

A child born into debt, a cost we never chose,
Just as we're told that for our sins, Jesus arose.
Why must we worship under threat of despair,
When love unconditional is what we're told to share?

I can't imagine Jesus would demand such a cost,
Nor that salvation is forever lost.
Why paint him as stern, demanding and cold,
When compassion and kindness are the stories we're told?

I honor the faith that others hold dear,
But I won't be shackled by doctrine or fear.

For heaven on earth is a dream we can weave,
Living with purpose, not living to grieve.

Why do they make Jesus seem so mean,
Worship or else, in torment unseen?
If everlasting life is what's guaranteed,
Why paint a savior with such a harsh creed?

Is love not meant to be freely given,
Not chained to threats of a fiery prison?
A soul's worth isn't by fear to glean,
Nor bound by doctrines that make love obscene.

I don't believe a strong heart needs all to kneel,
To feel tall or to make its love real.
A savior's strength is in lifting the weak,
Not in demanding the humbled and meek.

Yet I respect those who find their peace,
In faith's embrace, where their doubts cease.
For certainty's comfort is a gift they hold,
While I seek my truth, my own soul's gold.

In the end, we walk our paths unique,
Some need answers, others seek.
And though I question, I still hold dear,
The hope of a love that conquers fear.

Just Tell Peaches

I grew up where the sounds of the projects hummed,
Where roaches bungee jumped off your shoelaces for fun.
Where corner stores sold icy dreams,
And if you had a few sisters, you had a team.

We weren't rich, but we were built from fire,
Protected by Peaches — the original live wire.
She was the sixth of nine, a mix of sugar and boom,
She'd light up a room or flip one, too.

She'd flip the switch in a heartbeat's flick,
Kick your ass, then serve you quick —
Cook you dinner with a smirk and sigh,
With the steak she gave you to put over your eye.

We had all kinds in the neighborhood mix,
The dumb one, the snitch, and the one who'd slick-fix.
Ty was loyal, but dumb as a post,
He'd help hide the stash, then forget what we stole.

Black was the ringleader, fresh and bold,
Designer down but still always stole.
He'd say "let's just grab one candy bar," and boat
And leave with half the register stuffed in his coat.

Me? I was cautious — soft with nerves.
But one day, I let temptation curve.
I didn't steal, not technically true —
I squeezed the ice cream, let some leak through.

Just enough to taste — a drip on my hand,
Then BOW! — I got punched by the store clerk, DAMN!

I walked home crying, heart all bruised,
Until Peaches saw me and lit the fuse.

She stomped in that store, jaw locked tight,
And told that man, "My brother don't steal — get it right."
No questions asked, no side to pick,
Next thing I knew, I had a fresh new lick.

Same with Precious — she got caught red-handed,
Green icy in hand, wide-eyed and stranded.
Store clerk yelling, threat in his tone,
But Peaches showed up — and he left her alone.

"My niece don't need to steal from you!"
She barked, and the logic just felt true.
Precious walked out with her icy intact,
No money exchanged, no looking back.

Although on crack she commanded respect,
Unsecured lines with no credit check.

Peaches became legend — not just a name,
But a presence that played life like it was a game.
She fought drug dealers and never got pressed,
Her credit was fists and you know the rest.

Now adult life hits like a punch in the chest —
Like damn, y'all could've warned me
before I stepped into this mess.
I waited impatiently to grow up and become a man,
Only to wish for my childhood again.

The bills, the drama — y'all can have that shit back.
I'll take Atari and ass whippings than to try to race with these rats.

Hamster wheel on full spin cycle…

Then I moved to the South expecting a new scene,
I run into racism — that shit was in full steam.
And it's not coming from where you think it might seem,
It ain't coming from people — it's coming from things.

So I'm at Food Lion, keepin' it light,
Self-checkout lane, tryna do it right.
I scan two items — system FREEZE.
"Please wait for assistance." Like I'm tryna steal cheese.

Associate walks over, scans her badge,
Tryna play it cool, but I feel that glance.
It kept happenin'. Every few things —
The machine would stop like I'm stealin' wings.

Then I looked up — caught the view,
Overhead footage… zoomed-in too.
And there I was — caught in the frame,
Scan in hand, but lookin' insane.

Because on that screen, plain as day,
Was the rolls in the back of my neck on display.
All bunched up like hidden contraband,
Lookin' like a whole pack of ballparks tucked under my glands.

She looked at me like, "This man ain't slick,"
Like I snuck whole a picnic under my shit.

And I could tell she really ain't know what to say,
Like, "Is he shopliftin' or just built that way?"

Then she scanned one last time, gave it grace,
But the screen went BLACK — like it quit the case.
No total. No beep. No place to pay.
Just a long-ass receipt slid out my way.

It read: **"PAID. $0. BALANCE DUE."**
I hadn't even tapped — I swear it's true.
At the very bottom — printed neat,
In fine little letters at the edge of the sheet…

"JUST TELL PEACHES WE TOOK CARE OF YOU :)"

And right then I knew…
Peaches ain't a sister, ain't a person you call.
Peaches is energy — Peaches is law.

She don't break in — she overrides.
She don't explain — she rectifies.
She don't knock — she just appears…
And suddenly all your accountability disappears.

Barber From the Bronx,

~30 Years of Fades, Fools and Funk

I started out young, just 14 years old,
Clippers in hand, tryna get that gold.
Back in 1995, with a chair and a dream,
Takin' on clients who'd make grown men scream.

The old heads? Nah, they ain't trust the kid,
Had to take the lil' ones—cryin', flinchin', throwin' fits.
And the grandpas too, with the wispy thin hair,
Talkin' 'bout "Make me look young." Uh... Sir... where?

But I got nice wit it—real smooth with the fades,
Had so much time on my hands,
I learned to cut my own hair like a blade.
Got my own waves spinning, tight line-ups precise,
But Imma keep it be real... I done messed up once or twice.

Like that one time, oh boy, what a sight,
My first blowout, man I just couldn't get it right.
And in my defense this was my first try,
But the result made a grown African man cry.

Real authentic tears dripping down his strong face,
Had his ancestors looking down on him in disgrace.
But Moe Dread limped over and came thru with the save,
'Cause I had that man looking like the only option was a shave.

And then you got the cheapskates that come to the shop,
Crumpled-up fives, change clinkin' non-stop.
"Yo, can I get a taper?" Man, what you mean?
You can get a bus ride home and try to chase your dreams.

And don't get me started on the crackhead clique,
"Hood Entrepreneurs" out there thinking they slick.

They'd try to sell you a bike, a coat, and a clock,
Hell, one dude tried to sell me one loose pair of socks.

"Come on, big dawg, these fresh as can be!"
Bruh, they look like they walked here without any feet.

And dude was a felonious Muslim committing this sin,
Lookin' like he robbed a lost and found bin.

Another one came with just one walkie-talkie,
Who the hell am I gonna talk to with one walkie-talkie?

And the shape-up scam? Oh, that shit used to have me tight!
"Yo, just hit the sides…" Nah, nah you ain't right.
"You mind evening this out? Hit the eyebrows, too?"
Bruh, you booked a shape-up, not a spa day for you!

Yo, I swear these cats be plotting,
You can't make this shit up!
It's like they use shape-up as a trial version
Of a full haircut!

But the worst? The moms—oh Lord, here they come,
Hoverin' like I'm preppin' for open-heart surgery on their son.
"Don't push his hairline back!" Then I have to retort—
Your son's hairline is running from him,
I'm just here for moral support.

Then there's the breath—got a few with that breath,
A silent shop is a sign of distress.

If I ain't crackin' jokes, if the convo is dead,
Just know somebody's rectum is attached to their head.

This one dude said "hey" and I had to step outside,
Had to check if my porta-potty tipped over and died.
His breath was a force—some sort of nuclear blast,
It smelled like his soul was decomposing fast.

Needed to ask if he wanted enhancements, but a brutha was caught—
Even if he was about to say something,
I could smell this dude's thought.

I tried to be slick, and put the blade on his stache,
And asked him real light,
"Yo, you want fibers?" — mistake of my life.

His "Mmm hmm" hit me like a spiritual slap,
Had to turn him to the door, 'fore I collapsed.

I kept it to myself, didn't want to be mean,
But I wanted to hook dude to an IV that dripped Listerine.

You can't make this shit up!

But through all the years, the fades and the fakes,
The scammers, the hustlers, the breath that could bake…
I wouldn't trade it, not even a bit,
30 years in, and I'm still with the shits.

They say success is the best revenge.
But revenge for what, exactly?
That thing nobody said?

Imaginary ~~Friends~~ Enemies

They said I couldn't do it.
Who's "they"?
You mean them?
Over there?
The folks minding they business,
Not even thinking 'bout you?
Cool.

Because I don't recall a crowd
Forming outside your dreams
Holding picket signs that say
"YOU SHALL NOT SUCCEED."
I missed that rally.

Nobody told you no.
You just needed someone to blame
For why you waited so long.

Success feels heavier when it's earned.
Lighter when you frame it
As revenge on people
Who weren't even watching.

We've made "they"
A motivational crutch.
An imaginary opponent
To shadowbox in public
Until we feel heroic.

But truth be told —
There's no villain in this origin story

Except the version of you
That hit the snooze button on purpose.

Your struggle is real.
But your opposition?
Might just be a ghost you fed
To make your victory feel loud.

Win because you must.
Not because "they" said you can't.
Do it because it's divine,
Not because someone doubted you.

You ain't proving them wrong.
You're proving yourself late.

So stop giving "they"
Front row seats
To a show they never bought tickets to.

WHEN THE GRASS
OUTGROWS THE
DANDELIONS,
Wisdom whispers: even
weeds yield to time.

The Standard

She is the standard, the model, the queen,
The purest of souls—or at least that's the scene.
The woman of virtue, the mother, the prize,
A beacon of grace in her children's eyes.

But tell me, what's the standard when love turns to war,
When words cut like razors, yet she's keeping the score?
She swung first with venom, but that's never in view,
Only daddy's reaction is captured as truth.

She ripped through my pride, she spat on my name,
She disrespected me deep—but that's not in the frame.
No mention of how she betrayed and deceived,
How she twisted the knife and just watched me bleed.
No talk of the hurt that led to my yell,
Just daddy got angry, so now I'm in hell.

Our child only sees that I raised my voice,
Not the pain that she caused, not the lack of a choice.
Not the words that she hurled, the damage she did,
Just "Mommy looked sad, and Daddy got big."
So now I'm the monster, the beast, the disgrace,
While she wipes a generated tear from her innocent face.

I stood in my pain, I let anger arise,
I spoke from the hurt, I did not terrorize.
I didn't tower, didn't threaten, didn't even advance,
But the moment I raised my voice—I never stood a chance.

And trust me, I hate that I stepped out of line,
That I let her betrayal bring fury to mine.
That I lost my composure, that I let myself break,

That my voice held the rage that I swore I'd forsake.
But nobody else gets to judge me for that,
Not when they ignore what pushed me to snap.
That work is for me, that weight's mine to bear,
I am self-aware—I don't need them to stare.

Now I'm the villain, the beast in the tale,
While her sins are concealed behind a delicate veil.
She plays the martyr, the victim, the saint,
Her hands look so clean with the stories she paints.

She is the standard, the moral elite,
But tell me, is virtue still virtue when it's soaked in deceit?
She praises restraint, yet she picks at the wound,
Then gasps at the blood when the tension's ballooned.

And outside this home, it's the same masquerade,
Where standards for men and for women are played.
She posts thirst traps but demands men behave,
And on the 'Gram, publicly drools at prints through the gray.
Yet let a man mirror that same energy,
He's a creep, he's disgusting, he's lost all dignity.

She is the standard, the one men must chase,
A king in his kingdom still begging for grace.
Court me, adore me, work hard to be mine,
But another man's touch requires no time.
I take her to Ruth's Chris, for some obligatory ass,
SN gets the backseat— I'm the only one that's tasked
With keeping the passion alive,
Jumping through hoops just to lay by her side.

The hypocrisy stands like an unshaken tower,
A walking oxymoron drunk off her own power.
I loved her, I gave her my heart, my hand,
Only to find that she draws her own lines in the sand.

She bends every rule and justifies the price,
Oh yeah, she's definitely the standard… TWICE.
The damn **double standard.**
But let me shut up before I get crucified again.

Peace

In Between the Echoes,

In between the echoes,
he's not what they caption.
Not the sum of her sighs
or the screenshot of one rough
night.

He is what he fixes alone.
What he builds when no one is
watching.
He is sweat on the floor
after everyone sleeps.

They won't write poems for that—
but he still writes anyway.

He Left the Light on For Us

He didn't come from quiet—
he learned to make peace with it.
Grew up in a house where voices cracked ceilings
and fists left more memories than fathers did.
But even then,
he found music in the madness,
rhythm in the rage.

He was not a saint.
Had debts he never paid back.
Regrets he rarely named.
There were days he forgot to call his mother,
nights he loved the wrong woman right,
mornings he stared too long at the mirror
wondering what part of him
still needed fixing.

But still—
he built.

He wrote verses in margins of overdue bills,
painted peace between double shifts,
held dreams with dirt under his nails.
He was tired,
but tireless.
Quiet,
but convicted.

He didn't ask the world to forgive him—
he just worked to give it something worth remembering.

He wasn't loud,
but his choices were.
He made truth louder than trauma.
Made purpose louder than pain.

When his children asked where he went,
his wife would smile soft and say,
"He's out there trying to make the world feel something—
without breaking it more than it already is."

He laughed,
he cussed,
he forgot birthdays,
he showed up anyway.
He was human—
just like the art he left behind.

And when he died,
they found journals full of poems
and notes to people he never sent.
They found blueprints for songs,
letters to sons he didn't have,
prayers for daughters he never met.

He never needed to be seen.
He just needed to be felt.
And now he is.

He left the light on for us.

Pressure Is My Element

In the quiet before the storm, I lay my plans,
Blueprints drawn with careful, steady hands.
Though pressure is my element, I never take it light,
I prepare and I practice, deep into the night.

But when the moment comes, and the stakes begin to climb,
That's when I shine the brightest, that's my perfect time.
For all the preparation somehow leads to this:
Pulling magic from my pocket, turning pressure into bliss.

A jack of all trades, with a thousand hats to wear,
Never taking it for granted, always striving to prepare.
Yet in the final moments, when the pressure's at its peak,
That's when I find my rhythm, that's the magic that I seek.

From comedy to concerts, from the stage to the street,
It's the pressure that perfects it, makes every act complete.
Like my mother before me, making something out of none,
I thrive under pressure, that's how battles are won.

So here's to the moments when the stakes are at their peak,
When pressure shapes diamonds, and brings out what we seek.
In this dance of life, every twist and element,
I stand tall and proud, for pressure is my element.

The work is done.
The shoulders drop.
The breath deepens.
And finally, the mind begins to wander—
to something soft, something sacred.
A game beneath the stars,
where memory runs the bases,
and joy slides home.

Beneath the Black Diamond Skies

~A Dream Walk Through Black Baseball History

When sleep comes like a wind through a cracked window,
I slip into a place where the chalk lines glow.
The field is dark, but alive with ghosts.
And the hum begins… like the MRI that knows me best.

In the hum of the MRI, I journey through time,
To ballparks and legends that forever shine.
From my mother's gentle teaching to my father's Mets pride,
Baseball became my heartbeat, my guide.

From Rube Foster's vision to Bud Fowler's early trail,
They laid the foundation so strong and so hale.
Moses Fleetwood Walker, the first to play and stand tall,
While William Edward White passed as white—not breaking that wall.

Satchel, Cool Papa, and Double Duty Radcliffe,
Heroes whose stories give our spirits a lift.
Larry Doby in the American League, the first to break through,
Kurt Flood's fight for free agency, paving the way anew.

Buck Leonard's bat was thunder, pure grace at the plate,
A Hall of Fame hitter whose legacy holds weight.
And Buck O'Neil, the ambassador, voice of the past,
Kept their stories alive so their glory would last.

He swung, he coached, he spoke with pride—
The soul of the Negro Leagues still at his side.
Judy Johnson, a glove like a whisper, smooth and wise,
Fielded grounders like prayers beneath open skies.

Oscar Charleston? Power, speed, and soul,
Five tools on fire, a diamond made whole.
Leader and scout, a commander of men,
Whispers say he was better than all of them.

Josh Gibson, the Black Babe Ruth, they said with pride,
But truth flipped it—Ruth was the white Josh on the other side.
A bat like thunder, numbers off the charts,
He played for a people, and he played with heart.

And Babe Ruth—yes, we'll say it plain,
The Sultan of Swat walked a broader lane.
He didn't protest, didn't preach from the stage,
But his actions spoke loud in a segregated age.

He played exhibitions with legends barred from the show,
Dapped up greatness when the league said no.
And in photos—clear as day—what the world tried to shun,
He kissed Black children, hugged Black men like kin, like one.

No flinch, no fear, no hiding in the frame,
Just a man who honored talent, not a skin tone or name.
While others clung to lines that kept us apart,
Ruth saw the game—and the people—by heart.

He didn't need banners, didn't march with a sign,
But stood with our heroes, toe to toe on the line.
So in this long story, he's more than a myth,
He's a man who respected the soul of the riff.

Let us not forget Weldy Walker's name,
Moses' brother—part of that same flame.

The second Black man to play pro ball's stage,
Together they lit hope on a segregated page.

And far from the diamond, yet right in the fight,
Was Octavius Catto, who stood for what's right.
Before Jackie swung or Fleetwood took base,
Catto risked it all for his people's place.

He fought for the field, for dignity's claim,
A martyr whose story should echo the same.
Because freedom's a team sport, not a solo score,
And Catto swung hard from the civil rights floor.

And Jackie—before he wore forty-two on his back,
Took a stand in the Army, defying the pack.
In '44, court-martialed for staying in place,
Refusing to move from a white-only space.

Before Rosa sat, before marches began,
Jackie showed us what it means to stand.
Black history in baseball—always ahead,
Civil rights in cleats, long before it was said.

And then came Aaron—steady hands, thunder's grace,
The man who chased Ruth and redefined the race.
A Negro Leaguer turned MLB king,
With every home run, he made freedom sing.

And Willie Mays—the Say Hey Kid with soul,
Made center field a museum, turned defense into gold.
He ran like jazz, caught like scripture, swung like breeze,
Black joy in motion, doing it with ease.

They weren't just stars—they were the bridge,
From barnstorming fields to stadium ridge.
From the Negro Leagues' dust to televised prime,
Their greatness echoed through every time.

If I ever had a son, I'd name him just right—
Aaron Mays, for the swing and the flight.
Two legends, two flames, stitched in my name,
Living proof that greatness don't need fame.

So this isn't just names—it's legacy in verse,
A chorus of legends who shattered the curse.
In the hum of that MRI, their stories replay,
Black ballplayers who made a new way.

It's Not Crickets, It's Cicadas

It's not crickets.
It's cicadas—
sounding like sirens in a whisperless world.
You call it noise.
I call it testimony.

They weren't idle underground,
they were becoming.
Years in the dirt,
swaddled in silence,
crafting symphonies in their skin,
tuning instruments of bone and breath
for a concert no one invited them to.

They emerged
not to live—
but to be heard.
To rupture the quiet
with a life
they'd rehearsed
in roots and rot.

Just like us.
Buried in doubt.
Hidden in labor.
Tinkering with dreams no one asks about,
writing songs we may never sing aloud,
because the world only listens
after you're gone
or glowing.

You think it's just a racket,
but that's legacy
in surround sound.
A final creative crescendo
before they vanish
like artists
who spent a lifetime
becoming the loudest version of themselves—
just before they died.

It's not crickets.
Crickets are content.
This is the cry
of a soul that waited too long to be anything but quiet.

Big Ass Gardener

They say clear your mind…
But mine came with weeds.
Thoughts wrapped tight —
like unruly seeds.

Every day's pruning —

Snip, clip, repeat,
Snip — clip — repeat.
Fading the chaos…
But roots run deep.

In the shop I'm sharp —
Precision, no doubt.
But up here?
Some knots…
just don't come out.

Clients talk struggles,
while I blend and shape,
But behind that fade?
I'm fighting my own escape.

"Freezy, you cold."
Yeah — I play my role.
But behind the sharp lines?
I'm soothing my soul.

Some days get heavy.
Stress on overload.
Had to relieve some stress…
So I found me a new hoe.

Built me a haven,
right there in my yard,
Broccoli, beans,
Tomatoes on guard.

Okra standing firm,
Eggplants holding it down,

Cucumbers laid back
like they own these grounds.

Radish?
Speeding.
"Slow down, lil' man."
Mint?
…That one had plans.

See — mint's sneaky.
Left alone, it'll spread.
It don't care for boundaries —
just takes over instead.

And ain't that like worry?
Let it roam, it'll creep.
Fill every corner
till your mind can't sleep.

So I potted that mint.
Gave it walls to stay in.

'Cause boundaries ain't weakness —
They're where healing begins.

I'm out there daily,
gloves, boots, no shame,
Talking to peppers —
calling them by name.

Karen's on vocals,
Barry's smooth notes,
Mama Cass whispering —
while I check my growth.

Meanwhile —
outside?
Things falling apart.
Leaders orange as my carrots
Playing fake smart.

Ports closing down,
Shelves running low,
But I'm pulling up onions like:
"I'm good, bro."

Moms grew tomatoes
from a sill in the sky,
Bronx bricks to basil —
that hustle don't die.

Now I grow patience,
Grow laughter and ease,
While my daughter devours
the broccoli I please.

Patience in petals,
Healing in rows,
Joy in the quiet,
Peace as it grows.

I'm sharp with the blade,
But soft in the heart,
'Cause tending yourself?
That's the ultimate art.

So yeah…

I'm just a big ass gardener.

Big ass gardener…
…with dirt on my boots,
And love in each part.

So when they ask:
"Freezy, you still cuttin' heads up tight?"

I grin and reply:
"Yeah… but by night?
I'm a big ass gardener —
clipping negativity under moonlight."

Roots in the soil,
peace in my plan,
And YOU?
Better plant something too, fam.

'Cause nobody's delivering joy to your door,
but dig deep enough…
and yours will pour.

School molded the child—silence sculpted the soul.

Spiritual Audit

I pulled my soul's receipts today—
Faith deductions, karma credits,
blessings I never cashed.
Turns out grace don't roll over.

There were prayers marked "read"—
Ego, invested heavy—ROI pending.
I tithed my time to
people who overdrew my peace.

I tried to write off rage
as a spiritual expense—
but I couldn't prove it fed me.

Guilt? Filed under "miscellaneous."
Love? Claimed whole, delivered halfway.

I owe.
Not heaven. Not hell.
But myself—
for every time I skipped truth to feel better.

Now I balance
what's left.
No spiritual loans.
Just me.
The books.
And the breath to make it right.

We Were Safe in 55

~A love letter to the ones who mixed my paint shade by shade

There was something holy about that orange brick building.
C.E.S. 55.
Not across town. Not uptown. Not in a gated district.
Right there, where we lived, and where we learned to live.

It sat in the middle of the projects,
right across the street from my godmother's apartment at 1420.
So close, I could sleep over on school nights.
Closer than my own building—just a few doors down.
And across the other street? Saint Paul's Church.
That's where I went to Head Start.
My first classroom, my first lesson in life.

And somehow, in the height of the crack era—
in the ashes of burned-out buildings and broken promises
from the Civil Rights Era—
we were safe inside of 55.
We were loved.

Miss Grant had salt-and-pepper hair,
a heavy frame, and delicate, beautiful hands like my mother's.
Her presence alone made us sit up straight.
We were scared of her,
but it was the kind of fear you felt for God or Grandma—
a reverent fear.
And if you were lucky,
you learned she was gentle, soft-voiced, protective—
a mother during school hours.

Miss Lee?
Mean as hell when we were kids.
She popped me more than once, and I didn't mess with her.

But years later, when I brought my daughter to school,
we'd sit and talk about life—money—discipline.
She taught me more in that office than some books ever could.
She saved every tax return.
Didn't need it. Didn't touch it.
That's how she built wealth.
She passed not long after.
I miss her.

Then there was Miss Minnie Johnson.
Always in heels. Always polished.
Not just beautiful—presentable, every single day.
She called us "ladies" and "fellas."
Never "boys" and "girls."
She taught us how to be gentlemen.
She tied our good behavior to manhood,
and made us proud of chivalry.
She called me a vegetable because I never did my homework.
And when my niece Lulu did it for me,
she acted like she was having a Fred Sanford heart attack:
"Oh Lawd! Mr. Freeman did his homework!"

I couldn't hold the lie tho.
Told her the truth.
She didn't believe me at first,
but when she realized Lulu really did it,
she gave me a choice:
treats for the fellas, or no homework all week.
You can guess which way the fellas convinced me to go—
Of course I bought my homework away.
That's where I learned that honesty earns you options.

Miss Cordaro was my 6th grade teacher.
Italian lady. Softest voice. Always said *"Excusez-moi."*
She gave us treats. Made us feel seen.
Retired and passed not long after.
It broke my heart.

There was Miss White—Black woman from the projects just like us—
who ran the summer camp called Project Pride.
Back then, I thought it was just about being proud of the projects.
Later, I realized: We were the project.
It was a mission. A movement.
To put pride in us.
And she did.

Mr. Boyle—the gym teacher with a jump shot.
Young white dude who didn't just teach—he played with us.
5-2, knockout, horse—whatever we needed, he was game.
He was cool. He cared.

The lunch lady—God, I wish I remembered her name—
called us "Sugar Plum," "Sweetie Pie,"
like we weren't little dusty, snot-nosed kids.
She gave us sugar in our spirits.

Ms. Prichard and Ms. Richard.
Funny how close their names were.
Ms. Richard was the mean one.
Ms. Prichard? A whole different energy.

She played the witch every Halloween—and she looked the part—
but she was the sweetest soul in the whole school.
She walked through the projects like she was from there.
Old white lady, no fear, no front.
Bodegas. Courtyards. Kids yelling out her name:
"Hi Ms. Prichard!"
Hugs from grown-ups who used to sit in her classroom.
She didn't just teach us.
She belonged to us.

And Ms. Ramirez—how could I ever forget her?
She was like a big sister.
Puerto Rican, young, full of life.
She talked to us like people, not just kids.
And sometimes her mother who was the school secretary
would call on the loudspeaker
to remind her she forgot to wash the dishes.
We all cracked up.
She was human. And home.
She made 55 feel like a family.

Then there was Mr. Steinklein.
Not just an art teacher—an architect of imagination.
I never got to thank him.
He taught my sisters before me, and stayed all the way through mine.
He taught me that art was a voice.
That it belonged to us too.
He passed too young.
And I still dream about walking back in those doors,

reading one of my children's books aloud,
watching his face light up,
just to say:
"You made me a poet, sir. Thank you."

Ms. O J Davis,
My very first teacher.
Kindergarten.
She saw what I was made of.
Not just smart. Brilliant.
I could read better than some grownups.
She made me valedictorian.
She gave me the mic and I delivered that speech like it was the
Gettysburg Address.
Because of her, I knew:
I was supposed to shine.
She read *Swishy Tale* with us.
And I've been searching for that book ever since—
trying to give it back to her spirit.
Trying to say,
"Look, I never stopped reading."
My daughter Journey Jane?
She got that gene too.
Ten times sharper than I ever was.
I call her Journey's "grand-teacher."
Because Miss Davis lit a flame in me that still burns in her.

Ms. Cutler, the nurse,
taught me to clean myself up with pride.
Old white lady who gave good advice

and made sure we didn't walk around funky.
She didn't see color—she saw students.

Ms. Rafaela Lopez was technically the attendance lady,
but she was my guidance counselor.
Her love was abundant. Her listening was medicine.

Mr. Plummer, the principal—marched with Dr. King.
Carried that dignity in every word.
He died a year after I graduated.
But he lives in me.
They all do.

And then there was the library—
not grand in size, but grand in spirit.
A bigger classroom dressed up like a universe.
Mr. Clark held court there,
with bushy eyebrows you could probably cornrow
and a quiet, almost bashful energy.
When kids didn't drink their milk at lunch,
he'd collect the leftover cartons
and guzzle them down one by one—
his big Adam's apple bobbing up and down with every gulp.
We'd get a kick out of watching it,
the rhythm of it,
like he was swallowing clouds.
Some kids joked, but I didn't.
That was my place.
That was where I started researching.
Where my curiosity had room to roam.
Where I fell in love with the idea

that stories could live forever.
That facts had flavors.
That knowledge could feel like freedom.
Mr. Clark never had to say much—
his presence was a passport.
And that little library
was the greatest place in the world.

The murals on the walls of 55 told us our history.
1800s dates in bold letters.
Harriet. Frederick. Malcolm. Martin.
Heroes looking down from the walls, whispering,
"You are not forgotten."
And we believed them.

I used to walk those halls slow on purpose.
Not to skip class, not to be slick—
but to absorb it all.
On bathroom breaks I didn't need,
or just pausing mid-errand like I had somewhere to be—
I'd stroll past those glossy floors,
flawed but shining like somebody cared.
The hallways were wide, enormous,
like cathedral corridors carved for children.
And I could feel something in the air.
Something sacred.
It was in those walks that I learned to love Black history—
that I saw the numbers 1865, 1929, 1968
and started to piece together the stories.
It connected me to my father,
who was born in 1915,

and the quiet truth that my grandparents had lived in the 1800s.
I learned that history wasn't far away.
It was in the bricks.
It was in me.

We walked those halls with our heads high,
carrying the weight of ancestors
and the hopes of teachers
who gave their entire lives to us.

And because of them?
I probably never needed middle school.
Never needed high school.
Never needed college either.
Everything I ever needed to survive,
to build,
to love,
to rise—
I learned before I turned twelve.

I learned it all
inside the safe, beautiful walls
of **C.E.S. 55.**

The Artist Who Created in Silence

He never asked for applause.
Never waited for his name to be called.
He spoke through brushstrokes,
through rhythms,
through rhythms no one knew he wrote.

He walked through the world like smoke—
present,
but never trying to fill the room.
He moved like moonlight:
soft,
but still shaping the tide.

You didn't see him at the galas,
didn't hear him beg for likes.
But you've lived in his lines.
You've wept in his words.
You've stood taller
because something he made
told you to.

He never shouted,
but everything he touched echoed.

A quiet storm,
he poured meaning into moments
and let the silence
sing.

He drew strength from shadows,
power from purpose,
and left fingerprints

on the souls of strangers
without ever needing to be seen.

Legacy wasn't his goal—
Truth was.
Freedom was.
Healing was.

He didn't care if they remembered him.
Only that they remembered
what mattered.

And when they finally asked,
"Who created this?"
the answer came like wind through trees:
Someone who understood
that being loud
ain't the same as being heard.

Legacy in Silence

Some of the loudest lives leave the quietest echoes.

"What's remembered is never really gone."
— *Freezy the Barber*

In the Workshop of Memory

When I'm in my own company, I ponder life's long quest,
Knowing one day I'll lay down for my eternal rest.
No fear in my heart, but a gentle, deep dread,
For the ones I'll leave behind, the tears they might shed.

I think of my children, the legacy I leave,
In memories and moments, in the love they receive.
To be the best memory, a smile when they recall,
The joy, the warmth, the magic of it all.

Each Christmas tree adorned with memories so sweet,
A tapestry of moments, where past and present meet.
I cherish every second, for time is but a loan,
And one day I'll return to the place we all call home.

Though I no longer fear it, I still hold it at bay,
For there's so much to live for, so much left to say.
I'll leave this world better, with no stones unturned,
In the hearts of my loved ones, my lessons learned.

And when that day comes, when my work here is done,
I'll embrace the eternal slumber, like the setting sun.
No enemies, no regrets, just peace and love's ember,
To be the best memory, for them to remember.

The room didn't get cold—
you just took the warmth
with you.

For the Ones Who Left Too Early

They didn't miss life—life missed them.

Pretty Bird

A poem for Oowey

Pretty Bird, our Robin in flight,
A spirit so fierce, a soul so bright.
With fists of steel and a heart of gold,
She faced the world, defiant and bold.

From the streets where she reigned, a fearless queen,
To the soft moments in between.
A protector, a fighter, with laughter so sweet,
The girl with the chapstick, a memory we keep.

She was Robin, Oowey, our pretty bird, soaring so high,
A name that held magic we'd only learn by and by.
She danced to the rhythms of Caribbean seas,
An American rude gal, as fierce as the breeze.

She fought till the end with a will to survive,
A warrior's spirit, so fiercely alive.
But fate, it seems, had another plan,
Though we'll never understand, we hold tight to her hand.

In my garden, she lingers, unseen but near,
A rustle of feathers, a feeling sincere.
She shows up in moments both quiet and loud,
A breeze on your neck, a break in the cloud.

When I hear that chirp or feel that gust,
It's her saying, "I'm here, in spirit, in trust."
Not gone, just flying in a wider sky,
Still watching her people, still soaring high.

She left behind fire, compassion, and grace,
You see it in smiles, remembering her face.
In sisters who fight, in brothers who care,
Her legacy's stitched in the love that we wear.

ChapStick so sweet,
The flavored kind your little brothers used to sneak and eat.
To you it was chapstick
To us it was a treat.

And Journey Jane… she never hugged you in the flesh,
But video calls made the bond nonetheless.
You'd light up her screen with that one-of-a-kind Oowey smile,
And she still says she misses you once in a while.

She made amends like only Oowey could—
Beat you down one year, then love you for good.
Even her fiercest rivals showed up that day,
Leanin' over her casket like, "Ain't no way."
One kissed her forehead, tears in her eyes,
Like they came just to confirm she'd really died.

'Cause Oowey was a Washington Ave legend—
Cute enough to charm you, tough enough to check you.
She beat half the block and still had 'em smilin',
Left a trail of stories that keep on flyin''.

She made peace with God, and she made peace with them—
A full-circle soul who loved to the end.

So if you feel broken, if life takes a turn,
Think of our Robin, and what we can learn.
To love without limit, to live without shame,
To leave this old world with a powerful name.

"What I thought was a setback was just the universe holding the door until I had all the right pieces."

—*Freezy the Barber*

My Friend Bernie

Miles apart in age and worlds apart in time,
A Bronx-born artist meets a soul from another clime.
A friendship unexpected, through pages it did start,
A century's difference bridged by the magic of art.

He, a child of the twenties, with wisdom in his gaze,
Still played tennis at a hundred, full of life in countless ways.
I, a Bronx-born dreamer, with stories yet untold,
Found a friend in Grandpa Bernie, with a spirit young and bold.

From spider webs and butterflies to Martian tales so grand,
We brought his dreams to life, with a pen and steady hand.
His tears of joy, his laughter, that affectionate little tap,
A century's worth of memories wrapped in our creative map.

And when that first meeting ended, like a boy he stood so still,
Watching through the glass door, his heart with wonder filled.
"So long, James," he whispered, with a twinkle in his eye,
A moment of pure connection that neither time nor distance could deny.

So here's to Grandpa Bernie, whose legacy will stay,
In every line and illustration, forever on display.
Though miles and years may part us, our bond will never fade,
So long, dear friend—your art is lovingly laid.

Author's Note

Bernie Ditchick wasn't just a centenarian artist — he was my friend. Though we were 60 years apart, he insisted I call him Bernie from the moment we met. "Please," he'd say, waving off the formalities with a twinkle in his eye. We spoke like old friends, checked in on each other's birthdays, and over the course of 11 years, built a bond that was as real as any I've ever known.

He was sharp, witty, and so down to earth — not just a man from another time, but a spirit who could still reach across generations. Together, we brought his stories to life, sharing them with students in classrooms who were blown away to hear they came from a 90-year-old author. Bernie even spoke to them sometimes — and you could hear the pride in his voice.

He once wrote those tales for his grandchildren. I just had the honor of giving them wings.

Rest well, my friend.
– James

Borrowed Time
We walk like forever but breathe on a loan.

My Mom's Sister
(Sisters by Choice)

In Norfolk, Virginia, Moms began, a tale so rare,
Born to a duo, a mix-matched pair.
A white mom, a Black dad, but soon set free,
At ten days old, to a new family.

But Aunt Ann from Carolina came,
Different roots, different name, but oh, the same flame.
Though not by blood, their bond was tight,
Two sisters in spirit, shining so bright.

They laughed and cried, stood side by side,
When one faced storms, the other was the guide.
Mom had twelve, Aunt Ann had her crew,
They had seven kids each, side by side like a synchronized debut!

Who does that? you ask, with a grin,
"Let's have kids together!"—where to even begin?
From laundry to cookouts in that Bryant Ave lot,
Every moment together, the best that they got.

Through thick and thin, they raised their clan,
Like a dynamic duo with a lifelong plan.
Who needs shared genes when you've got shared dreams?
They redefined what sisterhood means.

And oh, that "tiddy bear," how Ann would say,
We'd laugh till we cried, in the funniest way.
They loved their gossip over butter rolls and coffee brew,
Two peas in a pod, forever true.

To Turk and Duke, now with them above,
We send our whispers, our endless love.
Though life took turns, they're all together,
Forever in our hearts, their bond won't sever.

Ann loved her red, like a blazing fire,
A hard worker to the end, never to tire.
From laundromats to hospitals, she worked to the bone,
Giving that apple cider wisdom, straight to the throne.

While Mom loved lavender, gentle and sweet,
Ann brought the heat, no lukewarm retreat.
She'd tell it like it is, with a no-nonsense flair,
The real truth you needed, with love and care.

To Lisa, Rat, Princess, Dodo, and Mike,
We love y'all deeply, more than words strike.
Though time moves on and roads may bend,
We're cousins for life—family 'til the end.

So here's to Aunt Ann, and Mom up above,
Two forces of nature, united in love.
Though not by blood, but by every measure,
They were sisters forever, a priceless treasure.

"Blood may start the story, but love writes the legacy."
— *Freezy the Barber*

Mommy's Message

Once a girl — pink cheeks, wide eyes —
With no clue of what's to be,
An adventure awaited, exceeding all imagination
One couldn't begin to foresee.

Inserted in a place and time,
And no one knows why.
But question not my God,
For duty called and work is to be done,
And I must earn and receive my nod.

Alma — means *nourishing soul.*
I did not choose my name,
But somehow God entrusted me,
So *nourisher* I became.

Sowing seeds and raising them —
Believe I did my best.
I loved you hard and gave you gems,
Now you must do the rest.

I loved my life through joy and pain,
Triumph and defeat.
And through everything that came my way,
Not once did I retreat.

My children, my children, my dear children,
You all must know the score.
For I know you'll miss me there on Earth,
But my father needs me more.

You'll get the storms and get to see
The beauty of rainbows — that's what this life often does.
And all I ask is, like me,
You do your best to leave this place better than it was.

Celebrate my life and all I've done,
Though I understand that this is painful.
But take comfort in knowing that forever and ever,
I will be one of God's angels.

So you'll never have to rest without me.

I love you all,

Love, Mom

Author's Note

This poem is written in my mother's voice—Alma Mae Mack—a woman whose name literally means *nourishing soul*. Though she never knew the meaning herself, she lived it every day. She poured love, wisdom, and discipline into her twelve children, and into everyone fortunate enough to know her.

Mommy's Message is my way of imagining what she might say to us now—her final letter of love, strength, and gentle instruction. I believe she *did* receive her nod. And while we miss her deeply, we know she finished her race with grace, purpose, and an unshakable faith.

One of her signature sayings was **"Rest with all God's angels."** She said it often—to her children, grandchildren, anyone she loved. It wasn't just a farewell—it was a blessing. That's why those words found their way into this poem.

Her legacy lives on in all of us. This is her message.

—Freezy the Barber

She Calls Me Daddy
For Winter
By Freezy the Barber

She calls me Daddy.
Not because she was told to,
but because love whispered it
first.
Not god-daddy, not uncle—just
Daddy—
like her spirit knew before she
could speak
that I would always pick up the
call.

She screams into the silence,
iPad propped on the pillow,
not facing me,
just needing to be heard.
And I sit in the stillness
like a soft place for her storm.

I tell her,
"Go clean your nose,"
like a code,
a gentle redirect
to bring her back to herself.
And it works—every time.

She lives states away,
but love don't do mileage.
It just shows up.
In the mail.
In the screen.
In the way she knows
who to call
when the world feels too loud.

And then—
"Daddy, can you buy me
snacks?"
No hello. No "how you doing?"
Just straight to the transaction.

I call her a snack digger—
little hustler with sugar dreams.
Toys too, of course.
Always plotting her next surprise
like birthdays come every
Tuesday.

But I show up.
Every time.
Because she's mine in soul,
not paperwork.
Because her love is loud,
and mine is louder.
Because she loves Journey
Because Journey calls her her
little sister—
Winter adores her
like she already understands
that love chooses family,
not the other way around.

Let other men count bloodlines.
I count answered calls,
carted toys,
sticky smiles,
and the way she says "Daddy"
like it's my real name.

Because it is.

Painting With Words

I never held a brush,
but I knew how to paint—
not in oils or pastels,
but in memory and truth,
in love and layered pain.

I paint with rhythm,
with breath between lines,
with the echoes of women
who built me from bricks and prayer,
with the silence of men
who never said much
but taught me everything
when they stayed.

I paint with the smile of my daughter
receiving simple flowers
like they were a galaxy.
With the voice of my mother
carried in a gospel note
or the hush before she spoke.

I paint with barbershop banter,
with street corner laughs,
with grief that don't come out smooth—
but jagged, like real life.

Each poem, a canvas.
Each line, a brushstroke.
Each story, a portrait
of a people who've learned
to keep breathing,
to keep blooming, to keep building joy
out of ash.

So if you see yourself in these pages—
your moms, your brother, your block, your burden—
know that it was by design.

I didn't write for perfection.
I wrote to remember.
I wrote to restore.
I wrote to reveal the beauty in the ordinary.

This is my gallery.
My legacy.
My way of saying:
I was here.
I saw it.
And I painted it... with
words.

Peace—Freezy

About the Author

James A. Freeman, known as Freezy the Barber, was raised in the Bronx during a time of cultural awakening and hardship—where hip-hop was born, crack hit hard, and community found its way through struggle. Growing up in the projects, he saw poverty and pain, but also joy, creativity, and love. Everything his family needed was there—bodegas, schools, churches, and basketball courts that transformed into outdoor concerts. Early hip-hop legends performed on the basketball court right outside his building, feeding the soundtrack of his childhood.

Without distractions like cable TV or digital screens, Freeman found wonder in books—especially a donated shelf of encyclopedias. He and his brothers explored history, baseball, and the legacy of their grandfather, a WWII veteran who died in 1946 from war-related causes when their mother was just a toddler. That curiosity lit a fire in him, further stoked by his mother—a Baptist soloist and poet—and by his art teacher, Mr. Steinklein. At age seven, he had his first poem published in a 1989 calendar. From that moment, poetry, music, and expression became his foundation.

Though much of his work draws from personal experience, his poems often speak to universal truths: the pain and triumph of women, the humor in cultural quirks, the resilience of brothers, and the beauty in being seen. He writes not for everybody, but for anybody—anyone who can find a reflection, a tear, a laugh, or a moment of truth in his words.

As a barber, Freezy considers his craft a form of art and healing. The barbershop becomes both stage and sanctuary—a space for listening, advising, storytelling, and reflection. He pours the same energy into poetry, blending his roles as therapist, artist, and entertainer.

Painting With Words is his first literary work for adults, following several acclaimed children's books he has written and illustrated. He believes poetry is a missing piece in both early literacy and adult expression—capable of opening hearts, ears, and imaginations. This collection, like his legacy, is meant to last. His art isn't for everybody—but it's for *anybody*. Anybody who needs to laugh, cry, reflect, or feel seen.

Acknowledgments

I've been writing poetry for nearly four decades, but it wasn't until this year that I found myself embraced by the poetry community. Performing, connecting, and growing — this season has shown me that it's never too late to come into your own.

I want to thank **Neil Donnell Ray**, a Fayetteville native and a force of poetic nature. For 27 years he's been building a community through music, art, and storytelling at *The Coffee Scene*. His voice is rich with history, and his presence makes you feel like you've always belonged. He welcomed me with open arms and helped me walk taller.

To my Art teacher **Mr. Steinklein**, who taught me that poetry is art — not just words on a page. You opened a world for me before I knew what world-building meant.

To **Aunt Lois (Dolores Macklin)** — my mother's best friend and my lifelong mother figure. You've loved me like your own and gave me that soft place to land my thoughts and feelings, even when I didn't know I needed it. You are the voice of truth, the extra hug, the realest heart in the room. I love you forever.

To **Lillie Mae Rojas**, my godmother and my second mom. You showed me structure, grace, and gentleness — even while running a house full of energy. At your home, I got to be the baby boy. Thank you for that gift.

To **Charlie Rojas**, my late godfather, thank you for showing me structure and for modeling Black love, partnership, and family. You showed me what unity looks like.

To **Morris Houses on Washington Avenue** — the projects raised me. Those blocks gave me everything: mistakes to avoid, lessons to live by, people to love. We were poor in money, but rich in life.

To **Charnay Phaire**, my brother in the barbershop and in the dream. You were the first college-educated brother to take me under the wing and expose me to the dream of black success —. To vision. To legacy. You were there for *"BBT"* before it was a poem or a punchline. I'm still laughing, still inspired. Still building.

To **the poetry community of Fayetteville, NC** — y'all are some of the most talented, raw, unsung artists in the country. This city is dripping with truth, rhythm, and brilliance. Don't wait for the world to validate you. Keep writing. Keep spitting. Keep building. The world needs us.

To everyone who ever poured into me, sat in my chair, believed in me, or said, "Keep going" — thank you. You helped raise this voice.